I0458319

FREEDOM FROM DISORGANIZED ATTACHMENT

THE STEP-BY-STEP GUIDE TO BUILDING SECURE RELATIONSHIPS AND LASTING LOVE

ELIZA BENNETT

CONTENTS

© Copyright 2024 Eliza Bennett — All rights reserved.

The content contained within this book may not be reproduced, duplicated, or transmitted without direct written permission from the author or the publisher. Under no circumstances will any blame or legal responsibility be held against the publisher or author for any damages, reparation, or monetary loss due to the information contained within this book, either directly or indirectly.

Legal Notice:

This book is copyright protected. It is only for personal use. You cannot amend, distribute, sell, use, quote, or paraphrase any part or content within this book without the consent of the author or publisher.

Disclaimer Notice:

Please note the information contained within this document is for educational and entertainment purposes only. All effort has been executed to present accurate, up-to-date, reliable, and complete information. No warranties of any kind are declared or implied. Readers acknowledge that the author does not render legal, financial, medical, or professional advice. The content within this book has been derived from various sources. Please consult a licensed professional before attempting any techniques outlined in this book.

By reading this document, the reader agrees that under no circumstances is the author responsible for any direct or indirect losses incurred as a result of the use of the information contained within this document, including, but not limited to, errors, omissions, or inaccuracies.

INTRODUCTION

In the quiet moments before dawn, Sarah lay awake, tangled in thoughts and sheets. Her mind raced with the fear that the man she loved might leave, though he lay sleeping beside her. She longed for closeness but felt a constant pull to push him away. This internal tug-of-war was exhausting. Sarah often wondered why love felt so complicated, why the fear of abandonment seemed to shadow every tender moment. Like Sarah, many find themselves caught in the web of disorganized attachment, a pattern rooted in early relationships that often leads to chaos in love and connection. This struggle, familiar to so many, inspired me to write this book.

My name is Eliza Bennett, and I have spent years navigating the complexities of attachment theory, both in my personal life and as a professional. I understand the struggles you might be facing because I have been there myself. My journey began with my own battles to appreciate my relationships, a struggle that I am sure many of you can relate to. This personal path, filled with ups and downs, has become a passion for helping others find clarity and healing. Through my research and writing, I have witnessed the profound impact of understanding and transforming attachment styles on people's lives. I am not just an author—I have walked a similar path and am here to guide you.

Disorganized attachment, a more common experience than one might realize, is a pattern marked by fear and a deep longing for connection. It often originates from inconsistent caregiving in childhood and can lead to challenges in adult relationships. The confusion and pain it causes make it a crucial issue to address, and it is essential to remember that you are not alone in this struggle. Many others, like you, are navigating this complex terrain.

This book offers a practical path forward. It is a step-by-step guide designed to help you shift from disorganized to secure attachment —a transformation that can significantly enhance your relationships and improve your emotional well-being. This book is for adults who recognize themselves in these patterns and seek change. It is for those tired of the cycle of fear and confusion who want practical, actionable solutions for real-life challenges. It is a guide that explains the problems those with disorganized attachment face and provides the tools to overcome it, empowering you to take control of your emotional well-being. With this book, you have the power to make a change.

Within these pages, practical guidance fosters a deeper understanding of your disorganized attachment style and equips you to build healthier connections. The chapters will cover, among other topics, emotional regulation, trust-building, and breaking toxic patterns, and each section is crafted to support your journey toward secure attachment. You will learn to navigate emotions, develop trust, and create lasting, fulfilling relationships. This book's unique blend of real-life examples, research-backed strategies, and practical exercises is designed to facilitate personal transformation. By integrating these tools into your life, you can experience genuine change.

I invite you to commit to this journey. Embrace the potential for positive change and the benefits of developing a secure attachment style. This book is about understanding disorganized attachment and creating a life filled with love and connection. Remember, you are not alone on this journey. I am here to guide you every step of the way, offering support and encouragement. As you turn these pages, remember that transformation is within reach. Let this book be your companion as you embark on a new chapter filled with hope and determination. We will journey to healing and secure, lasting love together.

CHAPTER 1
UNDERSTANDING DISORGANIZED ATTACHMENT

A YOUNG CHILD SITS QUIETLY IN A ROOM, TOYS SCATTERED AROUND them. Their eyes dart between the door and the clock, waiting for the moment their caregiver returns. But when the door finally opens, the child hesitates, unsure whether to run forward or stay still. This scene illustrates the complex world of attachment—the invisible bonds that shape our relationships from childhood through adulthood.

ATTACHMENT THEORY SIMPLIFIED

Attachment theory, a cornerstone of understanding human relationships, offers a lens through which we can view the dynamics of our connections. At its heart is the work of John Bowlby, who proposed that children are biologically predisposed to form attachments with caregivers. These bonds are crucial for survival. Bowlby's theory suggests that the quality of these early attachments influences how we relate to others throughout our lives. Mary Ainsworth, a key figure in this field, expanded on

Bowlby's work with her landmark "Strange Situation" experiment. A key part of this research observed how children responded to the presence and absence of their caregiver in a controlled environment, revealing distinct patterns of attachment behaviors. In this experiment, a child and their caregiver are placed in a room with toys. Then, the caregiver leaves the room, and a stranger enters. The child's behavior during these separations and reunions reveals distinct patterns of attachment behaviors. For instance, children with secure attachment styles could explore their environment when their caregiver was present, and they reacted positively when the caregiver returned after a brief absence.

This research revealed four distinct attachment styles: secure, anxious-resistant, avoidant, and disorganized. Each style reflects a unique approach to connecting with others, with disorganized attachment being the most complex and challenging pattern. These patterns shape how we approach relationships, handle conflicts, and experience intimacy. Understanding these patterns within ourselves can provide valuable insights. By understanding our attachment style, we can identify areas for growth and work toward healthier relationship dynamics.

Attachment theory is not just informative—it is transformative. It equips us with the knowledge to improve our relationships consciously. By applying attachment theory to our lives, we can strengthen our relationships. For instance, if you identify with an anxious attachment style, you might focus on building self-reliance and seeking reassurance from within rather than relying solely on external validation. This might mean trusting your partner's love and support in a romantic relationship without constantly seeking reassurance. In a work setting, it could mean taking on a challenging project without needing constant validation from your supervisor. If avoidant, you might practice vulnerability by sharing your feelings and thoughts with loved ones you trust. This could be as simple as expressing your feelings about a particular situation to a friend or family member. And for those with disorganized attachment, acknowledging the internal conflict and seeking consistency in relationships can be a step toward healing. This might mean seeking a supportive and consistent mentor in a work setting or maintaining a stable and supportive friendship. These practical applications of attachment theory empower us to make informed choices that foster security and connection, offering a hopeful path to healthier relationships.

Attachment theory also helps us understand our interactions with others and deepens our understanding of ourselves. It encourages us to reflect on our upbringing and how it continues to influence our adult relationships. More importantly, it provides a framework for change. By recognizing our patterns and tendencies, we can shift our attachment style toward one that promotes stability and fulfillment. This understanding is not about assigning blame or dwelling on the past but about using these insights to create a more secure and loving relational future. However, it is essential to note that attachment theory, like any psychological theory, has limitations. It primarily focuses on the relationship between a child and their primary caregiver, which may not fully capture the complexity of adult relationships. It also tends to be culturally biased, as it was developed based on research in Western cultures. But with this essential foundation, we can approach our relationships with empathy, understand the complex interplay of attachment styles, and be confident we have the tools to build the connections we genuinely desire.

THE NEUROSCIENCE BEHIND SECURE AND DISORGANIZED ATTACHMENT

The impact of attachment patterns is not just psychological—it is woven into the very structure of our brains. Modern neuroscience reveals how early relationships shape neural pathways, particularly in regions responsible for emotional regulation and social bonding. The amygdala, hippocampus, and prefrontal cortex—our brain's emotional command center—develop differently based on our attachment experiences.

In secure attachment, these brain regions work in harmony. The prefrontal cortex regulates the amygdala's threat response, producing balanced emotional reactions. However, in disorganized attachment, this neural dance becomes disrupted. Brain scans show heightened amygdala activity, suggesting an overactive threat-detection system. This explains why those with disorganized attachment might perceive danger in neutral situations or struggle to trust safe relationships.

The stress response system, regulated by cortisol and other hormones, also adapts to early experiences. Children in unpredictable environments develop hypersensitive stress responses that persist into adulthood. Their bodies maintain higher baseline cortisol levels, preparing for potential threats. This biological adaptation explains the hypervigilance and difficulty relaxing in relationships that many people with disorganized attachment experience.

The brain's plasticity offers hope, however. While early experiences create neural patterns, our brains remain capable of change throughout life. Consistent positive relationships and therapeutic interventions can reshape neural pathways. This process, known as neuroplasticity, means that new, healthier attachment patterns can be learned and integrated at the biological level. Understanding this biological basis helps validate the real challenges of disorganized attachment while affirming the possibility of change. This knowledge can inspire optimism and motivate us to work towards healthier relationships.

Recent research in interpersonal neurobiology shows how secure relationships can help regulate our nervous systems. Through "co-regulation," supportive relationships can help calm overactive stress responses and create new neural patterns for security. Co-regulation is how two individuals in a relationship, often a caregiver and a child, regulate each other's emotions. For example, a caregiver might soothe a child who is upset, which in turn helps the child learn to regulate their emotions. This biological perspective explains why healing often requires understanding our patterns and experiencing consistent, safe relationships that contradict our early programming.

THE ORIGINS OF DISORGANIZED ATTACHMENT

Imagine a world where a caregiver's embrace one day transforms into a cold shoulder the next. Such inconsistency leaves a child uncertain, unsure whether to seek comfort or brace for rejection. This unpredictability, often stemming from the caregiver's emotional struggles, teaches the child that relationships are inherently unstable. For instance, a child who witnesses domestic violence or experiences neglect may learn to associate closeness with danger. This creates a paradox where the child craves connection but fears the potential harm it might bring. The emotional unpredictability within the family environment reinforces this perception, making it difficult for the child to trust and feel secure.

The emotional state of the primary caregiver plays a pivotal role in shaping a child's attachment style. If a caregiver is preoccupied with their unresolved trauma, they may be unable to provide the consistent support a child needs. This can foster an environment where the child feels responsible for managing the caregiver's emotions, further complicating their understanding of healthy relational dynamics. The child may become hyper-aware of the caregiver's mood shifts, leading to heightened anxiety and a constant need to adapt to the caregiver's emotional state. Without consistent emotional support, these children develop survival strategies that, while protective in childhood, often complicate their adult relationships.

Without a secure base during childhood, we often struggle to develop a sense of safety in our adult relationships. A secure base is a reliable support figure who provides comfort and reassurance, allowing the child to explore the world confidently. Without this foundation, trusting others and establishing meaningful connections may be difficult. They may approach relationships cautiously, always on guard for signs of instability or abandonment. This can result in a pattern of pursuing relationships that mirror the unpredictability of their early experiences, perpetuating the disorganized attachment style into adulthood. Understanding these origins is crucial for breaking the cycle and moving toward the security and stability of healthier attachment patterns.

RECOGNIZING THE SIGNS OF DISORGANIZED ATTACHMENT IN ADULT RELATIONSHIPS

As children with disorganized attachment grow into adults, they often carry these early lessons into their relationships. The difficulty in trusting others can result in a constant push-pull dynamic, where the desire for closeness is frequently at odds with the fear of potential betrayal or rejection. Recognizing these signs in our adult relationships is the first step towards understanding and addressing disorganized attachment, empowering us to take proactive steps towards healthier relationships.

In adult relationships, disorganized attachment reveals itself through a tapestry of behaviors that confuse their partner. Emotional volatility is a hallmark of this attachment style. We might shower our partner affectionately one week only to retreat into cold detachment the next. This unpredictability can make relationships feel like a rollercoaster ride, leaving both people uncertain of the ground they stand on. Emotional regulation becomes a significant challenge, as we may struggle to manage the intense emotions that emerge due to perceived threats to our relationships. This difficulty often manifests as emotional volatility, where seemingly minor events can trigger profound reactions. This push-pull dynamic can be exhausting, leading to relationships fraught with tension and uncertainty.

We yearn for closeness yet dread the intimacy that closeness brings. This paradox manifests as a fear of abandonment, where the thought of losing a partner triggers intense anxiety. Simultaneously, there is a fear of engulfment, a worry that becoming too close might result in losing our identity or being overwhelmed by the relationship.

Trust issues also accompany disorganized attachment, further complicating relationship dynamics. We may overanalyze our partner's actions, interpreting innocent remarks or gestures as signs of betrayal or impending rejection. This constant scrutiny can erode the foundation of trust. As a result, there is often a reluctance to commit fully to the relationship, fueled by the fear that doing so might lead to inevitable heartbreak. The impact extends beyond romantic relationships into friendships, work relationships, and family dynamics. Each connection becomes an opportunity for either healing or reinforcing old wounds.

The impact of disorganized attachment extends beyond just relationships; it seeps into self-perception, leading to low self-esteem and chronic self-doubt. We may view ourselves as unworthy of love, attributing relationship struggles to personal shortcomings rather than recognizing the influence of their attachment style. This negative self-view can become a self-fulfilling prophecy, where believing our inadequacy leads to behaviors that sabotage potential happiness. As the years pass, this erodes confidence, making it even harder for us to trust our ability to maintain healthy, loving relationships.

Reflection Section: Recognizing Patterns

Take a moment to reflect on your relationship behaviors. Consider how emotional volatility, trust issues, or fears of intimacy and abandonment manifest in your interactions with others. Write down any recurring themes or patterns you notice. Acknowledge how these might relate to disorganized attachment. This awareness is the first step toward understanding and transforming your relational experiences.

REAL-LIFE EXAMPLES OF DISORGANIZED ATTACHMENT

Let us look at three different people with disorganized attachments. Let us begin with Alex, whose relationships often start with an intense connection, a whirlwind of passion and shared dreams. But as weeks turn into months, a creeping doubt takes root. He starts questioning their partner's intentions, scrutinizing every word and action for hidden meanings. Misunderstandings escalate into arguments, and Alex begins to pull away, convinced that retreat is safer than vulnerability. With Taylor, she oscillates between dependency and detachment. She relies heavily on others in friendships and romances for support and validation. Yet, when things become too intimate, she feels suffocated and fears the loss of independence. Taylor's relationships are characterized by intense closeness followed by sudden distancing. Finally, in the workplace, Tom's disorganized attachment hinders him. He excels in his role but struggles with teamwork. He perceives feedback as criticism and reacts defensively or withdraws from collaboration.

These real-world scenarios reveal how we find ourselves in relationships or situations that mirror our early inconsistent experiences. We may be drawn to partners who are emotionally unavailable or unpredictable or perhaps even misread situations. The result may be a relationship that feels like a battlefield, where both partners struggle to find common ground. Or we might interpret a partner's busy work schedule as a sign of waning interest, leading to accusations and defensiveness. Yet, as we will see in subsequent chapters, resolution is possible. Through self-awareness and open communication, we can begin to address these patterns.

THE ROLE OF TRAUMA IN ATTACHMENT AND THE ROAD TO HEALING

Trauma imprints a lasting impact on our psyche, influencing how we relate to ourselves and others. Imagine a child who learns that love can hurt when it should heal. Whether through witnessing domestic violence or enduring emotional neglect, these early experiences teach the child to associate closeness with danger or unpredictability.

The resulting hypervigilance manifests as constantly scanning the environment for signs of danger or betrayal, even when nonexistent. This heightened alertness stems from a survival mechanism honed in chaotic or threatening environments. Hypervigilance leads to misinterpretations of a partner's actions, seeing threats where none exist. Again, we oscillate between intense intimacy and sudden withdrawal. A partner may wonder why we pull away when things seem to be going well. Closeness can trigger memories of past trauma, leading to overwhelming anxiety. Understanding how trauma shapes attachment provides insight and opens the door to potential change.

The path to healing requires understanding trauma responses and developing new coping strategies. Recognizing the impact of trauma on attachment is crucial for recovery. Trauma-informed therapy offers valuable tools for this journey. (We explore therapy options more fully in Chapter 11.) Therapists understand the deep connection between past trauma and present attachment behaviors. They create a safe environment for us to explore their experiences without judgment, assisting them in unraveling these patterns. Practices like somatic experiencing or EMDR (eye movement desensitization and reprocessing) can help process traumatic memories.

Emotional regulation plays a pivotal role in trauma recovery. Developing emotional management skills is an essential step toward healing. Mindfulness, grounding techniques, and deep breathing can help us stay present and calm when we experience strong emotions. Developing emotional regulation skills also enhances relationship dynamics. In the next chapter, we will examine this in more depth.

CHAPTER 2

EMOTIONAL INSTABILITY AND EMOTIONAL REGULATION

IMAGINE STANDING IN A CROWDED ROOM, SURROUNDED BY THE HUM of conversation, when suddenly someone mentions your name in a critical tone. Your heart races, your palms sweat, and a flood of emotions threaten to overwhelm you. This is the power of emotional triggers—those seemingly small cues that can provoke significant emotional responses. They are often rooted in past experiences and deeply tied to our attachment styles. For those with disorganized attachment, these triggers can feel like invisible landmines scattered throughout their daily lives. But here is the key—understanding and managing these triggers is possible and a liberating step in fostering emotional stability, putting you in the driver's seat of your emotional journey.

UNDERSTANDING AND MANAGING EMOTIONAL TRIGGERS

Understanding and managing emotional triggers is crucial for those with disorganized attachment patterns. These triggers often stem from conflicting early experiences with caregivers, such as a caregiver who is physically present but emotionally distant or inconsistently responsive to the child's needs. This creates a simultaneous need for closeness and fear of intimacy, making emotional regulation particularly challenging in relationships. However, by understanding these contradictory impulses, we can empower ourselves to develop healthier attachment patterns and take control of our emotional journey.

Emotional triggers are stimuli that evoke strong emotional reactions, often disproportionately intense compared to the trigger itself. They can stem from sudden changes in plans, which may unsettle your sense of stability and control. Perhaps a friend cancels plans at the last minute, leaving you feeling abandoned or unimportant, reminiscent of past experiences of unpredictability. Criticism or perceived rejection is another potent trigger, striking at the heart of self-worth and stirring fears of inadequacy. Even a casually delivered remark can feel like a personal attack, sparking a cascade of defensive emotions. These reactions are not just psychological but physiological—activating the body's fight-or-flight response. This ancient survival mechanism floods the system with adrenaline, preparing you to confront or escape the perceived threat. While this response was invaluable to our ancestors, in modern settings, it often leads to overreactions and conflict.

Identifying your emotional triggers is the initial step toward managing them. A valuable tool in this process is keeping an emotional diary, where you can document situations that provoke strong emotions. Note the context, your immediate feelings, and any physical sensations you experience. Over time, patterns will emerge, revealing the specific triggers that disrupt your equilibrium. Reflecting on past conflicts can also shed light on recurring themes, helping you identify the roots of your emotional responses. This self-assessment requires honesty and introspection, as it involves confronting the vulnerabilities that underpin your reactions. But with this awareness, you gain the power to anticipate and prepare for your triggers, reducing their power over your emotions and putting you in control of your emotional well-being. This empowerment instills confidence in your ability to manage your emotional health.

While the physiological response to triggers is automatic, mindfulness can help us recognize the signs before they escalate. We can create a space between the trigger and our reaction by paying attention to our body's physical cues, such as a racing heart, clenched fists, or a tightening in the chest. This pause is an opportunity to choose a response rather than react impulsively. With practice, mindfulness can help retrain the brain to respond with greater calm and control, even in the face of triggers, allowing us to manage emotional responses more effectively. This sense of calm and control brings a profound peace to our emotional landscape.

Employing strategies that enhance emotional awareness to monitor and recognize real-time triggers is beneficial. Another practical approach is to engage in regular self-check-ins throughout the day. By setting aside a few moments to assess your emotional state and identify lingering tensions, you can cultivate a habit of self-awareness. This makes it easier to detect and address triggers as they arise. Visualizing a mental map of your emotional landscape can also help when you chart the connections between events, thoughts, and emotions. By mapping these relationships, you can better understand how different triggers are interlinked, allowing you to anticipate their effects more accurately and prepare for them.

Reflection Section: Identifying Your Triggers

Take a few moments to reflect on recent situations that provoked a strong emotional response. Write down the event, your emotions, and any physical sensations. Consider what might have triggered these reactions. As you review your notes, look for patterns or recurring themes. This exercise can help you pinpoint your triggers and develop strategies to manage them effectively.

MINDFULNESS TECHNIQUES FOR EMOTIONAL BALANCE

As we have seen, mindfulness practices are especially valuable for those overcoming disorganized attachment. They help build the internal stability often lacking due to inconsistent early caregiving experiences. By staying present, you can begin to trust your own emotional experiences rather than feel overwhelmed by conflicting impulses in relationships.

Think of moments when stress takes over, your mind racing with worries about work, relationships, or the future. In such times, mindfulness can offer a sanctuary—a way to ground yourself in the present and reduce the whirlwind of anxiety. At its core, mindfulness is about cultivating awareness of the present moment without judgment. It is a practice that invites you to observe your thoughts and feelings with curiosity rather than getting swept away by them. This simple yet profound shift can transform your emotional stability, offering a beacon of hope and optimism in your journey toward emotional balance.

Foundational Practices and Their Benefits

One of the most accessible mindfulness techniques is focused breathing. Focusing on your breath's rhythm can create a calming anchor amid chaos. This practice reduces stress and enhances your ability to regulate emotions by bringing you back to the present.

To embrace mindfulness further, you can also do a body scan meditation, which helps you connect with your physical self. Find a peaceful spot to lie down or sit comfortably. Close your eyes and then take a few deep breaths. Beginning at the top of your head, slowly move your attention down through your body, noticing any sensations, tension, or areas of relaxation. As you progress, breathe into each area, releasing tension with each exhale. For example, you might start by focusing on your forehead, noticing any tension or relaxation there, then move down to your eyes, cheeks, and so on until you reach your toes. This exercise fosters deep relaxation and awareness, helping you attune to your body's signals.

Another effective practice is mindful breathing. Sitting or lying down comfortably, close your eyes and focus on your breath. Notice the sensation of air entering through your nose, filling your lungs, and leaving your body. Gently take your focus back to breathing if your mind wanders. This technique cultivates patience and concentration, allowing you to respond to stress with better composure.

Mindfulness plays a crucial role in reducing emotional reactivity. When faced with a challenging situation, it is easy to react impulsively, allowing emotions to dictate your actions. Mindfulness introduces a pause, a moment to reflect before responding. This pause empowers you to choose a thoughtful response rather than being driven by immediate emotions. Over weeks and months, this practice can lead to a more balanced emotional state, where reactions are measured and intentional. Integrating mindfulness into daily life can weaken the automatic connections between triggers and responses, fostering a sense of control over your emotional landscape.

Consider the story of Emma, who struggled with overwhelming anxiety at work. Deadlines loomed, and the pressure felt insurmountable. Emma began incorporating mindfulness into her routine, dedicating ten minutes each morning to mindful breathing. Over weeks, she noticed a subtle shift. The anxiety that once paralyzed her began to dissipate. She became aware of the tension in her body, using her breath to release it. During meetings, when stress threatened to take over, Emma discreetly focused on her breath, finding calm amid the chaos. This newfound ability to pause and center herself transformed her work experience. Mindfulness became her ally, guiding her through stressful moments with a sense of peace and clarity.

Another story is that of Mark, who frequently argued with his partner. The most minor disagreements would escalate into full-blown conflicts. After learning about mindfulness, Mark decided to apply it during these heated exchanges. By focusing on his breath and observing his emotions, he learned to listen more and react less. Gradually, the arguments decreased, replaced by constructive conversations. Mark realized that mindfulness helped him communicate better and deepened his connection with his partner. These stories illustrate mindfulness's profound impact on emotional regulation, offering tools to navigate life's challenges gracefully and with understanding.

INTEGRATING MINDFULNESS INTO DAILY LIFE

Adding mindfulness to your daily routine does not require setting aside large blocks of time. It can seamlessly integrate into your activities, such as commuting or taking breaks. For instance, while commuting, whether you are driving, taking public transport, or walking, you can practice mindfulness by focusing on the sensations around you—the feel of the steering wheel, the rhythm of your footsteps, or the sounds in your environment. This practice helps reduce stress and makes your journey (in the literal sense) more enjoyable and less rushed. Similarly, during breaks at work, take a minute to center yourself. Close your eyes, take deep breaths, and release any tension. These small moments of mindfulness can break the cycle of stress and help you return to your tasks with a clearer mind and a calmer demeanor.

Introducing simple mindfulness practices into your routine can be straightforward yet profoundly impactful. Consider box breathing during work breaks. This technique involves inhaling for four counts, holding the breath for four, exhaling for four, and pausing again for four. Focusing on this rhythmic pattern can calm your mind, lower stress, and help you return to work with renewed focus. Similarly, mindful stretching before bed can help ease the day's tension, preparing your body and mind for restful sleep. This practice includes gentle stretches combined with deep breathing, encouraging relaxation and promoting peace as you transition into sleep.

Mindful walking offers another practice that can enhance daily life. Often, we move through spaces on autopilot, lost in thoughts about the past or future. Mindful walking invites you to focus on each step, noticing the sensation of your feet meeting the ground, the rhythm of your movement, and the environment around you. By engaging fully with walking, you create a meditation that grounds you in the present moment. This practice encourages you to slow down and connect with your body, transforming routine movements into mindfulness and stress relief opportunities.

Mindful transitions between activities offer another opportunity to integrate mindfulness. These brief moments, often overlooked, can be a chance to pause and reset. For example, when switching tasks at work, take a few deep breaths to clear your mind and refocus your attention. This simple act can increase concentration and smooth the transition, allowing you to approach the following task clearly and purposefully. These mindful pauses serve as mini-reset buttons throughout the day, helping you maintain a state of calm and attentiveness.

The benefits of regular mindfulness practice extend beyond the moments of calm they create. Consistent practice leads to sustained emotional balance, helping you respond rather than react to life's challenges. When mindfulness becomes a habit, you feel peaceful, even in the most chaotic circumstances. This emotional stability is not about eliminating stress or negativity but changing your relationship with these experiences. Mindfulness helps you learn to notice your thoughts and emotions without being swept away, which can contribute to a more balanced and less reactive emotional state.

Consider the story of Lucy, a teacher who found herself overwhelmed by the demands of her job. Between lesson planning and managing classroom dynamics, stress seemed unavoidable. Encouraged by a friend, Lucy started practicing mindfulness during her lunch breaks. She would sit quietly, focus on breathing, and let go of the morning's tensions. As time passed by, Lucy noticed a significant shift. She became more patient with her students and less frazzled by unexpected challenges. Mindfulness provided her with a sense of calm that permeated her entire day. Similarly, Jake, a software engineer, struggled with the fast pace of his work environment. He began using mindfulness while commuting, focusing on the present moment instead of worrying about the day ahead. This simple change transformed his mornings, making him more focused and effective at work.

Overcoming Challenges and Building Consistency

Despite its benefits, maintaining a mindfulness practice can be challenging. It is easy to forget or feel too busy to fit it into a hectic schedule. To overcome these obstacles, start small. Set realistic goals, like dedicating just five minutes a day to mindfulness. Gradually, as it becomes a natural part of your routine, you can extend the time.

Another common challenge is dealing with a wandering mind. It is typical for your thoughts to drift during mindfulness practice. If this occurs, gently bring your focus back to the present moment without judgment. Remember, the goal is not to clear your mind entirely but to cultivate awareness. For those with disorganized attachment, consistency in mindfulness practice can help establish the internal security that may have been missing in early relationships. This stable foundation becomes crucial when building new, healthier relationships.

Consider the story of Lana, a busy professional constantly overwhelmed by her hectic workdays. By incorporating mindfulness into her routine, she transformed her experience. Each morning, she practiced mindful breathing during her commute, setting a calm tone for the day. She used box breathing at work to manage stress, finding that these practices improved her focus and overall well-being. Then there is Jackson, a parent who struggled to be present with his children amid life's demands. By practicing mindful transitions, he learned to leave work stress behind and engage fully with his family. These practices made him more present, deepening his connection with his children and enriching their time together.

COGNITIVE RESTRUCTURING FOR EMOTIONAL HEALTH

In the tapestry of our minds, thoughts weave intricate patterns that shape our emotional landscapes. Cognitive restructuring is a technique that embarks on the journey of unraveling these patterns, offering a new perspective on how we perceive and respond to the world. This approach involves identifying negative thought patterns that often cloud our judgment and skew our emotional responses. Imagine, for instance, the belief that you are inadequate or unworthy. Such thoughts can trigger a cascade of emotions, leading to feelings of anxiety or depression. By challenging these thoughts and replacing them with balanced alternatives, you can alter the fabric of your emotional experience.

As discussed, those with disorganized attachment often struggle with contradictory thought patterns about relationships—simultaneously wanting closeness while fearing it. Cognitive restructuring can help identify and address these conflicting beliefs, making room for more secure attachment patterns. The process begins with recognizing these unhelpful thoughts, often termed cognitive distortions. These distortions include black-and-white thinking, catastrophizing, and overgeneralizing, among others. They can lead us to view situations exaggeratedly or inaccurately, impacting our emotions and reactions. Consider a scenario where a friend cancels plans, leading you to the immediate thought, "They must not value our friendship." This thought may not be grounded in reality, yet it can evoke feelings of rejection and hurt. Cognitive restructuring encourages you to pause and examine these thoughts critically. Are they based on evidence or assumptions fueled by past experiences?

Maintaining thought records can be incredibly useful in navigating this process. These records act as a tool to track and analyze your thoughts, helping you identify patterns and triggers. Start by jotting down situations that elicit strong emotional reactions and the thoughts and feelings they provoke. Next, evaluate these thoughts: Are they realistic? What evidence supports or contradicts them? This reflective practice lets you see your thoughts from afar, offering clarity and insight. As you become more adept at recognizing and challenging cognitive distortions, you can begin to replace them with more balanced, rational alternatives. For example, instead of thinking, *They don't care about me*, you might consider, *Perhaps something came up, and we can reschedule.*

Cognitive restructuring can profoundly impact emotional responses. Shifting thought patterns can transform how you react to situations, leading to healthier emotional outcomes. When you replace negative thoughts with balanced ones, you reduce their emotional charge, allowing you to respond more calmly and confidently. This shift enhances your emotional resilience and improves your interactions with others, fostering more positive and constructive relationships. Over time, cognitive restructuring enables you to cultivate a more reflective and less reactive mindset.

Engaging with exercises or scenarios can be beneficial to practice cognitive restructuring effectively. Consider creating worksheets that prompt you to dissect and reframe your thoughts. These might include sections for identifying the situation, noting the initial idea and emotion, and then challenging and revising the thought with evidence-based alternatives. Role-playing scenarios where you apply these techniques can reinforce your skills, helping you internalize the process. By consistently practicing cognitive restructuring, you can rewire your thought patterns, promoting emotional health and well-being.

Imagine the transformation of viewing life through a more transparent lens, where thoughts no longer dictate your emotional state but rather guide you with wisdom and balance. This transformation is not about ignoring negative emotions but understanding and reshaping the thoughts that underpin them. With practice, cognitive restructuring can become a natural part of your mental toolkit, equipping you to approach life's challenges more easily and clearly.

BUILDING EMOTIONAL RESILIENCE

Emotional resilience becomes particularly important for those healing from disorganized attachment as they learn to trust themselves and others. It provides the foundation to maintain healthy boundaries while allowing for genuine connection. Emotional resilience is the inner strength that enables you to recover from setbacks and adapt to change. Think of it as your inner compass that stays steady even when life gets stormy. It is like having an emotional immune system that helps you recover from setbacks and grows stronger with each challenge. When you develop this inner strength, you will find yourself surviving difficult moments and gaining wisdom from them. This capacity becomes your foundation for maintaining hope and direction, especially when your relationships or circumstances test your limits. For those working to build secure attachments, this resilience becomes particularly valuable—it helps you stay grounded in your worth even when old insecurities surface.

To enhance your emotional resilience, consider adopting a growth mindset. This involves viewing challenges as opportunities rather than threats, believing that abilities and intelligence can be developed through dedication and hard work. When cultivating a growth mindset, you become more flexible and willing to take risks. This mindset encourages you to embrace failures as learning experiences, which can significantly boost resilience. Engaging in regular self-care practices is another strategy to bolster resilience. This means prioritizing activities that nourish your body, mind, and spirit, such as exercise, relaxation, and hobbies. Self-care replenishes your energy. It enhances your ability to cope with stressors, creating a solid foundation for resilience.

Social support plays a pivotal role in building emotional resilience. Having a network of family, friends, or even colleagues who provide encouragement and understanding can significantly strengthen your ability to cope with stress. Feeling supported makes you more likely to persevere through tough times because you know you are not alone. Community and relationships provide a sense of belonging and security, essential to resilience. Nurturing these connections by reaching out, spending time together, and offering support in return is critical. Building and maintaining strong relationships can create a safety net that bolsters your resilience.

Consider the story of Mia, who faced the loss of a job she loved. Initially devastated, Mia leaned on her family and friends for support. She decided to view the situation as a chance to explore new opportunities. By adopting a growth mindset, she enrolled in courses to learn new skills. As months passed, Mia found a new job and discovered a passion for a different field. Her emotional resilience allowed her to navigate the challenge, learn from it, and emerge stronger. Then there is Jason, who faced a breakup that left him feeling lost. Instead of retreating into isolation, he joined a local hiking group, where he met others who shared similar experiences. The community offered understanding and companionship, helping Jason build resilience. He found comfort in nature and the friendships he formed, which provided him with the strength to move forward. These examples illustrate how emotional resilience can transform adversity into a stepping stone for growth.

Building emotional resilience is a dynamic and ongoing process. It involves actively engaging in practices that strengthen your ability to cope with stress and change. By nourishing a growth mindset, prioritizing self-care, and nurturing social connections, you can enhance your resilience and navigate life's challenges more easily. Resilience empowers you to face difficulties confidently and emerge from them with newfound strength and insight. As you develop this inner fortitude, you will find that you are better equipped to handle whatever life throws your way with a sense of calm and determination.

As we conclude this chapter on emotional regulation, we have explored various strategies to cultivate stability, from recognizing triggers to applying mindfulness in everyday life. These tools help you manage emotions and build a foundation for healthier relationships. Next, we will delve into trust-building and overcoming fears, paving the way for more secure attachments.

CHAPTER 3
BUILDING TRUST AND OVERCOMING FEAR

PERHAPS YOU FIND YOURSELF AT A CROSSROADS WHERE THE PATH OF trust seems obscured by shadows of doubt and past experiences. Trust issues often arise from deep-seated betrayals or broken promises that have left scars. But remember, these scars are not permanent. They are not the end of your journey but a part of it. Maybe you remember when a friend broke a promise or a partner failed to show up when it mattered most. These moments etch memories of disappointment, fostering skepticism about the reliability of others. As years pass, such experiences can harden into a protective shield that keeps potential pain at bay and blocks out genuine connections. The influence of parental relationships on our trust development cannot be understated. As children, our first lessons in trust often come from our caregivers. If those caregivers were inconsistent or unreliable, the seeds of distrust might have been sown early on, leading us to question the dependability of those around us. These experiences create a framework through which we view the world, making trust seem fragile and elusive. But remember, this framework can be reshaped, and trust can be rebuilt. The potential for growth and change is always within reach.

TRUST ISSUES AND REBUILDING TRUST PERSONALLY AND PROFESSIONALLY

Trust issues can have a deep-rooted impact on both personal and professional relationships. They can act as a barrier to forming close bonds, leaving you isolated even in the company of others. When trust is absent, misunderstandings become frequent companions, as suspicion clouds judgment and twists intentions. In friendships, you might question the motives behind a friend's actions, leading to tension and conflict. In romantic relationships, this suspicion can breed jealousy and insecurity, creating a cycle of doubt that erodes the foundation of love. Professionally, trust issues might make it difficult to collaborate or delegate tasks, as the fear of being let down overshadows the potential for teamwork and innovation. This pervasive sense of distrust not only damages relationships but also hinders personal growth, as it keeps you from fully engaging with the world around you. For those with disorganized attachment patterns, trust issues are often compounded by contradictory experiences with caregivers who were both sources of comfort and fear. This complicated history can make building trust incredibly challenging, as the desire for connection conflicts with the instinct for self-protection.

Recognizing signs of trust issues within yourself or others can be the first step toward addressing them. One telltale sign is a reluctance to share personal information, stemming from the fear that vulnerability might be exploited. You might find yourself holding back details about your life, keeping others at arm's length to protect your heart. Overanalyzing others' intentions is another indicator, where you scrutinize every word and gesture for hidden meanings or potential threats. This constant vigilance can be exhausting as the mind races to uncover betrayals that may not even exist. Such behaviors create an emotional distance that can be difficult to bridge, leaving relationships strained and unsatisfying.

To start restoring trust, it is crucial to engage in self-reflection. This introspective exercise is a powerful tool that puts you in the driver's seat, allowing you to delve into the origins of your distrust and examine the past experiences that have shaped your current perceptions. Reflect on moments when trust was broken and consider how these events have influenced your behavior and beliefs. This process of self-reflection is not about dwelling on past hurts but about understanding how they have shaped you. Ask yourself what assumptions you make about others' trustworthiness and whether these assumptions are based on present reality or past hurts. Journaling can be a powerful tool, letting you articulate your thoughts and feelings, creating clarity and insight. By understanding the roots of your distrust, you can dismantle the barriers it has built, paving the way for healthier, more fulfilling relationships. Self-reflection is a journey of empowerment and control, allowing you to shape your trust narrative.

Reflective Exercise: Uncovering Trust Challenges

Spend some time reflecting on a recent interaction in which you felt distrustful. Write down the situation, your thoughts, and the emotions it stirred. Consider what past experiences might have influenced your reaction. Identify any patterns in your responses to similar situations. This exercise is not about self-criticism but about gaining insight into how trust issues manifest in your life. By recognizing these patterns, you can start challenging and changing them. For instance, if you notice that you often question others' intentions, try to give them the benefit of the doubt. If you tend to hold back personal information, try sharing more with someone you trust. These small changes can help you overcome your trust issues, opening the door to a more trusting and connected future.

STRATEGIES TO BUILD TRUST WITH OTHERS

Building trust is a process that unfolds through consistent and intentional actions. One of the foundational techniques is active listening. This means being fully attentive and present to what the other person is expressing. It means setting aside distractions and allowing them to express themselves without interruption. Picture a conversation where you nod, maintain eye contact, and respond thoughtfully. This simple act of being present can profoundly affect how others perceive your trustworthiness. It shows them you value their thoughts and feelings and respect their right to be heard. Open communication complements active listening by encouraging honesty and transparency. Sharing your thoughts and feelings openly invites others to do the same, creating a reciprocal flow of dialogue that fosters mutual understanding and trust. Consistency is crucial here; when your words align with your actions, it builds a reliable foundation. Imagine the impact of consistently following through on promises or being punctual. Such actions reinforce the message that you are dependable, gradually strengthening the bonds of trust. When healing from disorganized attachment, consistency becomes exceptionally crucial. Small, reliable interactions help rewire the expectation of unpredictability that often characterizes disorganized attachment patterns. Each fulfilled promise, no matter how minor, helps build a new foundation of trust.

Vulnerability plays a pivotal role in deepening connections and fostering trust. You invite others into your world by sharing personal stories or experiences, offering them a glimpse of your authentic self. This openness can be daunting, but it signals trust and can encourage others to reciprocate. Consider when you revealed a challenging moment from your past to a friend or partner. The act of sharing not only deepens your bond but also demonstrates your willingness to be open and honest. This mutual exchange of vulnerability lays the groundwork for a trusting relationship. It is important to remember that vulnerability does not mean oversharing; it is about revealing parts of yourself safely and appropriately.

To practice building trust incrementally, start with small, manageable steps. Group settings, such as team-building exercises or workshops, can provide a safe environment to practice trust-building activities. These might include exercises where you share something about yourself, engage in a problem-solving task, or participate in a trust fall. Such activities foster a sense of camaraderie and collective trust. Setting small, achievable trust-building goals in your relationships is also effective. For instance, you might begin by sharing a minor concern with a friend and observing their response. Over a while, as trust grows, you can gradually open up about more significant issues. These incremental steps help build a strong foundation of trust without overwhelming either party.

Success stories of restored trust can inspire and offer hope. Take the example of a couple who decided to rebuild their relationship after experiencing a breach of trust. They began by committing to open and honest communication by dedicating weekly time to discuss their feelings and concerns. They slowly rebuilt their bond by practicing active listening and being vulnerable about their fears and hopes. After a few months, their relationship grew much more substantial, grounded in a deeper understanding and appreciation of each other. Another story involves a friendship that was tested by a misunderstanding. Through consistent efforts to communicate openly and share vulnerabilities, the friends were able to mend their relationship, ultimately emerging with a stronger connection. These narratives highlight the transformative power of trust-building strategies, illustrating that trust can be restored and relationships revitalized with patience and effort.

OVERCOMING THE FEAR OF ABANDONMENT

Imagine the lingering echo of a door closing, a sound that resonates deeply for someone with a fear of abandonment. This fear often has roots in past experiences, particularly those from childhood. Separation or loss during formative years can leave an indelible mark, teaching a child that love and security might be temporary. Perhaps a parent left unexpectedly, or a significant move disrupted a child's sense of stability. These moments can instill a fear that those you rely on could vanish without warning. As adults, we may relive these early separations through repeated relationship breakups, each one reinforcing the belief that closeness inevitably leads to loss. This pattern can lead to a pervasive sense of insecurity, where the fear of being left alone becomes a constant companion. For those with disorganized attachment, the fear of abandonment often coexists with a fear of closeness, creating a push-pull dynamic in relationships. This contradiction stems from early experiences where caregivers were simultaneously needed yet frightening.

The behavioral manifestations of abandonment fears are varied and can subtly infiltrate everyday interactions. You might find yourself clinging tightly to relationships, driven by an overwhelming need for reassurance. This clinginess can surface as frequent calls or texts, seeking constant confirmation of love and commitment. While seeking closeness is natural, it can suffocate both parties involved due to fear. Overdependence on partners for reassurance is another typical behavior—a reliance on others to validate your worth and dispel the fear of being left behind. This can manifest as needing constant verbal affirmations or requiring a partner to prove their dedication repeatedly. Such dependencies can strain relationships, as the burden of providing continual reassurance becomes exhausting over time.

Practical coping strategies can be invaluable in managing and reducing these fears. Developing self-soothing and grounding exercises is a powerful approach. These techniques help you regain control over your emotions in moments of panic or anxiety. As mentioned, taking deep breaths, focusing on the physical sensations of your body, or even engaging in calming activities like drawing or listening to music can anchor you in the present moment. These practices shift your focus away from the fear of what might happen to what is, providing relief from the grip of anxiety. As we have seen, cognitive reframing is another effective technique. It can alter how you perceive abandonment scenarios. It involves challenging and changing the negative thoughts that fuel your fears. Instead of assuming a partner's silence means they are leaving, consider other possibilities—they might be busy or need time to recharge. This shift in perspective can alleviate unnecessary worry and promote a more balanced view of relationships.

Stories of overcoming abandonment fears can offer hope and guidance. Consider Lisa, who struggled with the fear of losing her partner. She felt panicked whenever he went on business trips, convinced that distance would lead to disconnection. Lisa learned self-soothing techniques through therapy, like practicing mindfulness during absences. She also worked on cognitive reframing, reminding herself of the firm foundation of their relationship. As weeks passed, Lisa found that she could handle his trips with much less anxiety, focusing instead on their joyful reunions. Then there is Ben, who faced a similar fear after a series of failed relationships. He realized that his overdependence on reassurance stemmed from his lack of confidence. By engaging in activities that boosted his self-esteem, like joining a local sports team, Ben found he needed less validation from his partner. These narratives demonstrate that while the fear of abandonment can be deeply ingrained, navigating and overcoming it with understanding, patience, and the right strategies is possible.

SETTING AND RESPECTING BOUNDARIES

Boundaries serve as invisible lines that define where you end and others begin. You set the limits to protect your well-being, ensuring your physical, emotional, and mental needs are respected. Imagine boundaries as a personal space bubble, unique to each person that dictates how close others can get, literally and figuratively. They are crucial for healthy relationships because they establish clear expectations and prevent misunderstandings. Without boundaries, relationships can become enmeshed, leading to resentment and conflict. You communicate your values and needs by setting limits and fostering mutual respect and understanding. These boundaries empower you to take control of your personal space, allowing you to engage with others safely and comfortably.

Identifying and setting your boundaries requires introspection and clarity. A helpful exercise to begin with is journaling, which allows you to reflect on your limits and how they have been respected or violated. Start by writing down situations where you felt uncomfortable or overextended. Consider what triggered these feelings and what actions you wish had been taken differently. This reflection helps you pinpoint your boundaries, giving you a clearer sense of what you need to feel secure. Once identified, practice role-playing scenarios where you assert these boundaries with a trusted friend or therapist. This practice builds confidence, preparing you to communicate your limits effectively in real-life situations. By rehearsing these conversations, you become more comfortable expressing your needs, reducing the anxiety that often accompanies boundary-setting. For those working to overcome disorganized attachment, boundary-setting can feel particularly challenging due to inconsistent early experiences with limits. Learning to establish and maintain healthy boundaries becomes a crucial step in developing secure attachment patterns.

Maintaining boundaries can be challenging, mainly when others are resistant or push back against your limits. You might encounter people who dismiss your boundaries, viewing them as inconveniences rather than necessities. This resistance can come from a lack of understanding or a fear of change. In these instances, it is important to remain steadfast, reiterating your boundaries with clarity and calmness. Remember, boundaries are not about controlling others but about caring for yourself. You have the right to assert your limits, even if others disagree. It is also essential to be flexible, recognizing that boundaries might need to be adjusted over time as relationships and circumstances evolve. This adaptability ensures that your boundaries remain relevant and practical, reflecting your current needs and priorities.

Respecting others' boundaries is equally important and can enhance trust and satisfaction in relationships. When you honor someone else's limits, you respect their autonomy and individuality. This shared respect fosters a supportive environment where everyone feels acknowledged and appreciated. It encourages open communication, allowing for honest exchanges about needs and expectations. Recognizing and respecting boundaries builds a foundation of trust that strengthens your connection. This respect also empowers others to express themselves authentically, knowing that their boundaries will be honored. In turn, you create a relationship dynamic that is supportive and nurturing, where both people thrive in an environment of mutual understanding.

Reflect on boundaries and consider how they manifest in your relationships. Are there areas where your boundaries feel compromised, or do you struggle to respect others' limits? Explore these questions through introspection and dialogue, using the insights gained to foster healthier, more balanced interactions. By prioritizing boundaries, you cultivate relationships grounded in respect and trust, where each person's needs are valued and protected.

SELF-COMPASSION AS A TRUST-BUILDER

Imagine standing before a mirror, not to critique your reflection but to offer kindness to the person looking back. This is the essence of self-compassion, a crucial element in building trust with ourselves. It involves treating yourself with the same understanding and warmth you would offer a dear friend. When you embrace self-compassion, you cultivate an internal sense of security, laying the groundwork for trust. This practice of self-compassion is especially vital for those with disorganized attachment, as it helps create the internal security that may have been missing in formative relationships. This nurturing approach to ourselves can soften the harshness of self-criticism, allowing us to forgive past mistakes and see them as opportunities for growth rather than failures. By practicing self-forgiveness, we break the cycle of guilt and blame, replacing it with acceptance and learning.

Self-compassion plays a significant role in reducing self-criticism, which often acts as a barrier to personal growth. Many of us have an inner critic scrutinizing every action and decision, overshadowing achievements with doubt. By countering this voice with self-kindness, you can mitigate harsh self-judgment. Instead of fixating on perceived failures, self-compassion encourages you to focus on your efforts and intentions. This shift in perspective can be liberating, freeing you from the shackles of perfectionism. It allows you to recognize your inherent worth, independent of external validation or success. Through this lens, personal growth becomes a journey of exploration and acceptance, not a relentless pursuit of flawlessness.

To nurture self-compassion, consider engaging in meditations specifically designed to foster kindness toward yourself. Find a quiet space, close your eyes, and focus on your breath. As you breathe in, imagine filling yourself with warmth and acceptance. As you exhale, release any tension or judgment. Visualize yourself as you would a close friend, offering words of encouragement and support. This practice helps internalize a compassionate mindset, gradually replacing self-criticism with understanding. Another effective exercise is writing compassionate letters to yourself. In these letters, address your struggles and challenges with empathy and care. Acknowledge your efforts and reassure yourself that it is okay to make mistakes. Writing can reinforce inner dialogue, transforming how you relate to yourself.

Consider the story of Anna, who once struggled with debilitating self-doubt. She often felt paralyzed by the fear of making mistakes, leading her to avoid growth opportunities. Through self-compassion practices, Anna began to view her imperfections with kindness. She started each day with a self-compassion meditation that grounded her in acceptance. As the days went by, Anna noticed a shift in her mindset. She became more willing to take risks and embrace new experiences, trusting her ability to learn from setbacks. Similarly, David found himself trapped in a cycle of self-criticism that hindered his creativity. By writing compassionate letters to himself, David discovered a newfound freedom to express himself without fear of judgment. These narratives highlight the transformative power of self-compassion, illustrating how it can rebuild trust in yourself and unlock potential.

As you cultivate self-compassion, you create a foundation of trust within. This internal security empowers you to face challenges with resilience and courage. It also enhances your relationships, as the kindness you extend to yourself naturally extends to others. By nurturing self-compassion, you foster peace and confidence permeating all aspects of your life. This chapter has delved into the intricacies of trust, offering tools to build and sustain it within and with others. As we journey forward, we will explore strategies for breaking unhealthy relationship patterns, paving the way for deeper connections.

CHAPTER 4

BREAKING UNHEALTHY RELATIONSHIP PATTERNS

Picture yourself in a dimly lit room, searching for a way out. You feel along the walls, hoping for a door or a window, but all you find are more barriers. This is what it can feel like to be trapped in a cycle of toxic relationships. These patterns can be as elusive as they are damaging, often hidden beneath layers of emotions and interactions that, on the surface, seem ordinary. Yet, they can lead to a profound sense of entrapment, where the prospect of change feels like an unreachable dream. The first step toward breaking free is understanding what constitutes a toxic relationship and learning to recognize the signs.

IDENTIFYING AND PROCESSING RELATIONSHIP TRIGGERS

For those with disorganized attachment patterns, understanding relationship triggers is like turning on a light in a dark room. It often manifests as intense, seemingly contradictory reactions to intimate situations. These triggers can stem from early experiences where caregivers were simultaneously sources of comfort and fear. This understanding is crucial for breaking unhealthy patterns and developing secure relationships, and it can bring a sense of enlightenment to your journey.

Relationship triggers commonly surface in various situations that challenge our sense of safety and connection. When a partner becomes temporarily unavailable, it might trigger deep-seated fears of abandonment. Paradoxically, unexpected displays of affection can also become triggers, as they might feel threatening to those who learned early that intimacy could lead to harm. Conflict situations, particularly involving disagreement or criticism, often activate these triggers, as do moments of emotional vulnerability when sharing feelings. Even physical proximity can become challenging, as we feel uncomfortable when others are too close or distant.

When these triggers activate, we often experience a complex web of reactions. The most distinctive is the simultaneous urge to seek closeness while pushing away—a hallmark of disorganized attachment. This internal conflict can lead to emotional flooding, where feelings become overwhelming, or conversely, to emotional numbness, where feelings shut down entirely. Emotional flooding is when we become overwhelmed by one or more emotions. It can feel like a wave of intense feelings that is difficult to manage or control. Physical symptoms frequently accompany these emotional states, including a racing heart, shallow breathing, or feeling frozen. Many struggle to maintain present awareness, instead becoming lost in memories or future fears. The mind might race with conflicting thoughts about the relationship, creating a state of confusion and anxiety.

Processing these triggers requires a gentle, step-by-step approach. The journey begins with developing the ability to recognize triggers as they arise rather than getting lost in reactive patterns. This awareness creates space for implementing grounding techniques, such as focused breathing, progressive muscle relaxation, or physical anchoring to the present moment. Learning to name emotions without judgment helps create distance from overwhelming feelings, making them more manageable. As awareness grows, we can identify the core fears or needs underlying their triggers, such as the need for safety or fear of vulnerability.

Clear communication becomes essential in this process, though it often feels challenging. When possible, sharing these experiences with partners helps create understanding and support. This might involve explaining triggers beforehand or developing signals when feeling overwhelmed. However, it is equally important to recognize when professional support is needed, particularly when triggers feel too overwhelming to process alone. Whether through therapy, support groups, or trusted friends, building a support network provides crucial resources for this healing journey.

IDENTIFYING TOXIC RELATIONSHIPS AND PATTERNS

Toxic relationship patterns are often characterized by manipulative behaviors that undermine trust and respect. One such behavior is gaslighting, a form of psychological manipulation where a person seeks to make you doubt your perceptions or reality. This tactic can erode your sense of self as months or years pass, leaving you questioning your judgment. Emotional abuse is another hallmark of toxic relationships, manifesting through yelling, ridicule, or belittling. These behaviors can be subtle, cloaked in sarcasm, or disguised as jokes, but their impact is deeply corrosive. Emotional neglect, where one partner consistently ignores the emotional needs of the other, can be equally damaging. Emotional neglect can manifest in various ways, ranging from a partner consistently dismissing your feelings to a lack of emotional support during difficult times. It fosters feelings of invisibility and worthlessness. Recognizing these behaviors is crucial, as they often form the foundation of an unhealthy relationship dynamic. For those healing from disorganized attachment, toxic patterns may feel familiar or even comfortable, making them particularly challenging to identify and change.

The impact of toxic patterns on mental and emotional health is significant. Chronic stress becomes a constant companion, as the unpredictability of the relationship keeps you on edge. This stress can manifest physically, with symptoms like muscle tension or insomnia, and emotionally, leading to anxiety or depression. As time passes, these patterns can erode self-esteem, creating a cycle where the more you endure, the less worthy you feel. This erosion of self-worth can make it difficult to imagine a healthier relationship, trapping you in negativity and despair. The effects can be far-reaching, impacting your relationships and capacity to connect with the world.

Reflecting on your relationship history can illuminate patterns that might otherwise go unnoticed. This introspection is not about assigning blame but about gaining clarity. Consider keeping a relationship journal to document interactions, conflicts, and resolutions. This practice can reveal recurring themes or behaviors that contribute to the toxicity. Your relationship history includes all your past relationships, not just your current one. Reflect on past conflicts, asking yourself what triggered them and how they were resolved. Were there patterns of communication that perpetuated misunderstandings? Did certain behaviors consistently lead to feelings of hurt or inadequacy? This reflection can provide valuable insights, helping you identify the dynamics that need to change. To aid in this introspection, here is a checklist for identifying toxic patterns in your relationships:

1. First, consider whether you frequently feel drained or unsupported by your partner. Healthy relationships should be a source of mutual support and energy, not exhaustion.
2. Next, assess your communication. Do you find yourself reluctant to share your thoughts or feelings openly? This hesitation can indicate a lack of trust or fear of judgment. Evaluate the balance of power in the relationship. Are decisions made collaboratively, or does one person consistently dominate?
3. Finally, consider whether your boundaries are respected. Can you assert your needs and have them honored, or are they dismissed or ignored?

Use this checklist to diagnose unhealthy dynamics, bringing awareness to areas that need attention and change.

Interactive Element: Toxic Patterns Checklist

- Do you frequently feel drained or unsupported in your relationships?
- Are you reluctant to communicate openly with your partner?
- Is there a fair balance of power and decision-making in your relationship?
- Are your boundaries respected, or are they often dismissed?
- Do you experience manipulative behaviors like gaslighting or emotional neglect?

Recognizing toxic patterns is a decisive step toward breaking free from them. You can identify unhealthy dynamics by reflecting on your relationships and using this checklist. This awareness is a foundation for change and a powerful tool for making choices that foster healthier, more fulfilling connections.

TOOLS FOR BREAKING THE CYCLE OF TOXICITY

In the labyrinth of relationships, finding your way out of toxic patterns often begins with the cornerstone of establishing clear personal boundaries. As discussed in the previous chapter, these boundaries act as invisible guardrails, guiding your interactions and protecting your emotional well-being. They are not walls meant to isolate but guidelines that define what is and is not acceptable. To establish these boundaries, identify what makes you uncomfortable or unhappy in your interactions. Are there specific behaviors that consistently leave you feeling overwhelmed or undervalued? Once identified, communicate these boundaries clearly and assertively to those around you. Expressing your needs without ambiguity is essential, ensuring others understand your limits. When establishing boundaries seems challenging due to disorganized attachment, start with small, manageable limits that feel safe to enforce. This process is not a one-time event but an ongoing practice of self-respect and self-care, reinforcing your right to a healthy relational space.

Honest and open communication is another powerful tool in disrupting toxic cycles. It requires you to express your feelings and thoughts transparently, without fear of judgment or retaliation. This means engaging in conversations that might feel uncomfortable but are necessary for growth and understanding. Honest communication involves speaking your truth and being willing to listen—truly listen—to the perspectives and emotions of others. It is about creating a dialogue where both people feel heard and valued. This openness can dissolve misunderstandings and foster a more profound connection when practiced regularly, replacing toxicity with trust and respect. Remember, communication is a two-way street, and being receptive to feedback is as crucial as sharing your experiences.

The role of support systems in fostering change cannot be overstated. Breaking free from toxic patterns often requires the strength and perspective that a supportive network can offer. Understanding friends and family can provide encouragement and a sense of belonging, reinforcing that you are not alone in your journey toward healthier relationships. Turning to professional support, such as therapy or support groups, can be highly valuable. These resources create a safe environment to explore emotions, reflect on behaviors, and develop strategies for personal growth. A therapist can help steer you through complex emotions and equip you with tailored tools. In contrast, support groups foster connection with others who have faced similar challenges, offering mutual understanding and encouragement.

Engaging in exercises to practice healthier behaviors can reinforce your commitment to change. Daily affirmations are a straightforward but powerful way to bolster your self-worth and shift your mindset. Begin each day by affirming your value and potential, using statements that resonate with you, such as "I am worthy of love and respect" or "I choose to create healthy relationships." These affirmations can counteract the negative self-talk that often accompanies toxic patterns, gradually changing the narrative you hold about yourself. Role-playing difficult conversations is another practical exercise. By rehearsing these interactions, you can build confidence and prepare for real-life scenarios, ensuring that you approach them with clarity and calm. Such practice can help you navigate challenging discussions with poise, reducing the likelihood of falling back into old, unhealthy patterns.

Success stories of breaking toxic cycles can inspire and motivate, illustrating that change is possible. Take Elizabeth, who spent years in a relationship marked by manipulation and control. She found the courage to establish firm boundaries, clearly articulating what she would no longer tolerate. With the support of a therapist, Elizabeth learned to communicate her needs assertively and left the toxic relationship behind. Over time, she rebuilt her life, fostering new relationships grounded in mutual respect. Another story is that of James, who grew up in a family where emotional neglect was the norm. As an adult, he realized this pattern had seeped into his relationships, leading to unfulfilling connections. By joining a support group, James found a community that encouraged him to break free from these patterns. He practiced open communication and learned to express his emotions honestly, transforming his relationships into sources of joy and support.

These narratives, though unique, share a common thread: the power of intentional change. They demonstrate that by employing tools like boundaries, communication, and support systems, you can disrupt the cycle of toxicity. Whether through personal determination or with the aid of others, breaking free from unhealthy patterns is achievable and deeply rewarding.

EMPOWERMENT THROUGH SELF-AWARENESS

Picture yourself standing at a crossroads, feeling confident in your choice of direction because you understand your destination and the path that resonates with you. This clarity comes from self-awareness, a powerful tool that enables you to make informed and empowered relationship choices. When you are attuned to your personal needs and desires, you can navigate the complexities of relationships with a sense of purpose and confidence. Recognizing what you truly want from your connections allows you to set boundaries that protect your well-being and align with your values. This self-knowledge empowers you to enter relationships not from a place of need or uncertainty but from strength and clarity. It helps you identify what adds value to your life and what does not, making it easier to walk away from situations that no longer serve you.

Developing greater self-awareness often begins with introspection, which involves turning your focus inward to explore your thoughts, feelings, and motivations. Once again, mindfulness practices can be a valuable tool in this exploration, helping you observe your internal landscape without judgment. By regularly setting aside time to sit quietly and pay attention to your breathing, you can become more aware of the thoughts and emotions that arise. Notice patterns or recurring themes, and consider what they might reveal about your current state of mind. This mindfulness technique encourages you to remain in the moment, reducing the noise of external distractions and allowing you to connect with your genuine self. Keeping a self-reflection journal can further enhance this process. As you write, explore your daily experiences, challenges, and successes. Reflect on how they align with your core values and aspirations. This ongoing dialogue with yourself can illuminate your true priorities, helping you make choices that reflect who you are and what you want. For those with disorganized attachment, self-awareness allows us to recognize the push-pull dynamic in relationships and understand that reactions stem from past experiences rather than present reality.

Self-awareness also plays a crucial role in recognizing external influences and pressures that may impact your decisions. In today's fast-paced world, it is easy to be swayed by the expectations of others or the pressures of societal norms. By cultivating self-awareness, you can distinguish between your desires and those imposed by external forces. This discernment allows you to resist pressures that do not align with your authentic self, enabling you to make choices that are true to your inner convictions. For example, you might notice that a friend's opinion affects your decision about a relationship. With heightened awareness, you can step back and assess whether their influence aligns with your values or if it is causing you to act against your better judgment. This clarity helps you remain true to your path, fostering relationships built on authenticity rather than conformity.

The transformative power of self-awareness is profound, as it has the potential to bring about meaningful positive changes in your life. We can learn from the story of Emily, who realized that her constant need for approval was rooted in a lack of self-awareness. She began to understand her underlying fears and motivations through mindfulness and journaling. This insight allowed her to break free from the cycle of seeking external validation, giving her the confidence to pursue relationships that honored her true self. Similarly, Alex discovered that his tendency to avoid conflict was linked to a more profound fear of rejection. By cultivating self-awareness, he learned to face his fears and engage in open, honest communication, transforming his relationships and strengthening his emotional resilience. These examples illustrate how self-awareness can catalyze growth and empowerment, leading to healthier, more fulfilling connections.

As you embark on this journey of self-discovery, remember that self-awareness is a continuous process. It requires curiosity, patience, and a desire to explore the depths of your inner world. Embrace this exploration with an open heart and mind, knowing each insight brings you closer to the empowered, authentic life you envision. Self-awareness is key to unlocking your potential and creating relationships that reflect your best self.

BEHAVIOR MODIFICATION TECHNIQUES

Behavior modification is vital in personal relationships to foster healthier dynamics. At its core, behavior modification involves intentionally changing specific behaviors that may be contributing to relational discord. By focusing on altering these behaviors, you create a ripple effect that can transform how you interact with others, ultimately leading to more fulfilling relationships. Positive reinforcement is a cornerstone of this approach. It encourages desired behaviors by rewarding them, thereby increasing the likelihood of their recurrence. Imagine the satisfaction of receiving a genuine compliment or a small token of appreciation from a partner after a meaningful gesture. These positive reinforcements serve as powerful motivators, strengthening the behavior and increasing the likelihood that it is repeated.

To modify behavior effectively, setting achievable goals is crucial. These goals should be specific and realistic, providing a clear roadmap for change. Start by identifying a behavior you want to alter, such as improving your conversation-listening skills. Break this goal down into small, manageable steps, like committing to maintain eye contact or practicing active listening techniques. Focusing on one aspect at a time can build confidence and momentum as you progress. Another practical tool is the use of habit trackers. These can help monitor your progress by visually representing your efforts. Every day you successfully implement the desired behavior, mark it on your tracker. Over weeks and months, this visual record serves as a testament to your dedication, highlighting patterns and areas for improvement.

To further support behavior modification, engaging in exercises that reinforce new, healthier behaviors can be beneficial. Developing a reward system is one such exercise. This involves identifying rewards that are meaningful to you and using them to celebrate milestones. For instance, if your goal is to express gratitude more often, treat yourself to something special each time you reach a set target, like writing a thank-you note or verbally acknowledging someone's efforts. This practice not only incentivizes the behavior but also creates positive associations, making it more enjoyable. (We explore the role of gratitude further in Chapter 9.) Visualization is another effective exercise. Spend a few minutes each day visualizing successful interactions where you embody the behaviors you wish to cultivate. Picture yourself communicating with empathy and patience, and imagine the positive responses from others. This mental practice can enhance your confidence and prepare you for real-life situations.

The power of behavior modification is evident in stories of personal transformation. We can look at the case of Laura, who struggled with interrupting others during conversations. She recognized this habit as a barrier to deeper connections. By setting a goal to improve her listening skills, Laura began practicing active listening techniques and used a habit tracker to monitor her progress. She also developed a system of rewards, treating herself to a favorite activity each week she met her targets. Within a year, Laura noticed a significant change in her interactions. Conversations became more meaningful, and her relationships strengthened as others felt heard and valued. Another example is

Mark, who aimed to reduce his tendency to procrastinate essential discussions with his partner. Mark gradually overcame his avoidance by visualizing successful conversations and setting small goals to address issues promptly. These stories illustrate that altering relationship behaviors is within reach with determination and the right strategies.

Behavior modification is not just about changing actions but reshaping the way we engage with others. It empowers you to break free from patterns that no longer serve you, paving the way for healthier connections. As you embrace these techniques, remember that change is a process, and progress may be gradual. Celebrate each step forward and remain patient with yourself. Applying these strategies consistently can help you transform interactions and cultivate rewarding and resilient relationships.

With the tools and insights gained from behavior modification, you are well-equipped to navigate the complexities of relationships. Each step toward change contributes to a broader personal growth and connection journey. As we conclude this chapter, consider how these new behaviors can impact your life, setting the stage for deeper exploration in the chapters to come.

CHAPTER 5
CULTIVATING SELF-WORTH AND SELF-COMPASSION

THINK OF A MOMENT WHEN YOU FELT THE WEIGHT OF SELF-DOUBT pressing heavily on your shoulders. Perhaps it was after receiving criticism at work, or the whisper of inadequacy crept in during a social gathering. These feelings are all too familiar for many of us, and they can become a constant companion if left unchecked. Yet, there is a powerful antidote to this internal struggle: self-compassion. We touched on self-trust briefly in Chapter 3. This chapter will guide you through a deeper understanding and cultivating self-compassion, a transformative practice that can significantly enhance your mental well-being. For those with disorganized attachment stemming from inconsistent or unpredictable caregiving during childhood, developing self-worth can feel particularly challenging due to conflicting early experiences with caregivers. This chapter offers specific tools such as self-compassionate letter writing and daily self-kindness reflections to help rebuild a stable sense of self.

UNDERSTANDING AND CULTIVATING SELF-ACCEPTANCE AND SELF-COMPASSION

Self-compassion and self-acceptance are intertwined practices that form the foundation of healthy self-worth. Self-compassion is treating yourself with the kindness you would offer a friend, while self-acceptance means embracing your strengths and limitations without judgment. These two practices work hand in hand, with self-compassion providing the emotional support and understanding needed to accept oneself fully. For those healing from disorganized attachment, these practices become essential tools for establishing internal stability and breaking cycles of self-criticism.

Research, including Kristin Neff's work, shows that these practices positively influence mental health by reducing anxiety and depression. They involve three key components: self-kindness, recognition of common humanity, and mindful awareness. Accepting yourself fully while offering compassion for your struggles creates an internal environment that supports healing and growth.

The journey toward self-acceptance and compassion often faces barriers, particularly for those with disorganized attachment patterns. These might include fear of vulnerability, difficulty trusting yourself, and conflicting internal messages about self-worth. Overcoming these barriers involves building trust in your own experiences and emotions while learning to quiet the harsh inner critic that may have developed from inconsistent early relationships.

Interactive Element: Exercises to Cultivate Self-Compassion

Here are some practical exercises to help you develop self-compassion:

1. **Self-Compassionate Letter Writing**: This exercise involves setting aside time to write a letter to yourself, addressing a challenge or mistake with empathy and understanding. The key is to acknowledge your feelings and offer comfort and encouragement as you would to a dear friend. This exercise can shift your perspective and foster a more compassionate view of yourself, allowing you to practice self-compassion tangibly. It reinforces the idea that you are worthy of kindness and understanding, even in difficult situations.

2. **Daily Self-Kindness Reflections**: Each evening, reflect on your day and identify moments when you were self-critical. Consider how you could have approached these situations with more kindness and understanding. Write down your reflections and set an intention to practice self-kindness the following day. This practice is crucial to your journey toward self-acceptance. It fosters a more compassionate view of yourself and encourages you to be kinder to yourself.

These exercises can cultivate self-compassion and nurture a more supportive inner dialogue. This practice enhances your mental health and enriches your relationships and overall quality of life.

EMBRACING SELF-ACCEPTANCE

Picture yourself standing in front of a mirror, seeing your reflection and the essence of who you are, with all your strengths and flaws. This is self-acceptance. It means embracing yourself fully and acknowledging both your talents and your imperfections. Self-acceptance is crucial to personal growth because it allows you to live authentically without the constant pressure to conform to unrealistic ideals. When you accept yourself, you let go of perfectionism, understanding that having limitations and making mistakes is okay. This acceptance fosters a sense of peace, freeing you from the relentless pursuit of an unattainable standard of perfection and empowering you to live on your terms, feeling confident and in control of your personal growth.

However, achieving self-acceptance is often easier said than done. Many barriers stand in the way. One of the most significant obstacles is the fear of judgment or rejection. The worry about how others perceive you can be paralyzing, leading you to hide your true self. This fear often stems from past experiences where you felt judged or excluded, leaving a lasting impact that makes you cautious about revealing your authentic self. Internalized criticism from past experiences is another formidable barrier. Negative comments or failures can linger in your mind, creating a harsh inner critic that constantly undermines your confidence and self-worth. These internalized voices can be relentless, and viewing yourself with kindness and understanding is challenging.

To cultivate self-acceptance, it is essential to practice forgiveness for past mistakes. This means acknowledging errors without letting them define you or your worth. Instead of dwelling on what went wrong, focus on what you learned and how you have grown. Forgiveness allows you to release guilt and move forward with a lighter heart. Celebrating small victories and progress is another effective strategy. These "small victories" could be as simple as maintaining a healthy habit, completing a task at work, or showing kindness to others. Recognize and appreciate your achievements, no matter how minor they may seem. This practice helps shift your focus from shortcomings to accomplishments, reinforcing a positive self-image. By celebrating your progress, you build a foundation of self-worth that supports your journey toward acceptance.

We can learn from Michael, who spent years battling negative self-talk. He constantly compared himself to others, feeling inadequate and unworthy. Michael learned to challenge these thoughts through therapy and embrace his unique qualities. He began practicing daily affirmations and celebrating small victories, such as completing a challenging project at work or learning a new skill. Over the months, Michael found peace in his identity, realizing that his worth was not determined by external validation but by his acceptance. Similarly, Stacy struggled with accepting her body image after years of criticism. She started a journey of self-acceptance by forgiving herself for past mistakes and focusing on her strengths, like her creativity and compassion. Through mindfulness and self-reflection, Stacy learned to love herself wholly, imperfections and all.

These stories illustrate the transformative power of self-acceptance. Embracing who you are opens the door to personal growth and fulfillment. You become free to pursue your passions and live life on your terms without the constraints of societal expectations or self-imposed limitations. Self-acceptance allows you to build a strong foundation of confidence and resilience, empowering you to navigate life's challenges with grace and authenticity. As you embrace your true self, you cultivate an inner peace that enhances your well-being and enriches your relationships.

GRATITUDE JOURNALING FOR SELF-WORTH

Have you ever woken up in the morning with a sense of dread about the day ahead, your mind instinctively listing all that might go wrong? Now, picture starting your day differently—by focusing on what you are thankful for. A gratitude journal is a simple, powerful tool that can shift your perspective from focusing on flaws to recognizing strengths. By documenting daily moments of gratitude, you train your mind to seek the positive, fostering a sense of appreciation that boosts self-esteem. This practice is about shifting your focus from what you lack to what you cherish, reshaping how you perceive yourself and the world around you. Even in small doses, focusing on the good nurtures a more positive self-image and enhances your overall sense of self-worth. For those healing from disorganized attachment, gratitude journaling can help anchor positive experiences that might otherwise feel threatening or confusing.

Starting a gratitude journal is straightforward and requires only a few minutes daily. Begin by choosing a notebook that feels inviting—something you look forward to opening. Each day, write down three things you are grateful for. These do not have to be monumental; they can be as simple as the sun's warmth on your face or a kind word from a colleague. The key is to be specific, capturing what made those moments memorable. Regularly reflecting on these positive experiences can help cement them in your mind, making gratitude a natural part of your thought process. Over months and years, this practice can cultivate a habit of looking for the good in everyday situations, fostering a more optimistic and resilient mindset.

The psychological benefits of gratitude practices are well-documented and profound. Focusing on gratitude has improved my mood and fostered a more positive outlook. When you regularly write in a gratitude journal, you notice increased optimism and happiness. This change in perspective lets you approach challenges with a more hopeful attitude, believing in the possibility of positive outcomes. Additionally, gratitude enhances your sense of connectedness to others as you become more aware of the kindness and support present in your life. This increased awareness can lead to deeper, more meaningful relationships as you express appreciation for those around you, strengthening bonds and fostering mutual respect and affection.

Consider the story of Jane, who struggled with persistent feelings of inadequacy. She began gratitude journaling at the suggestion of a friend, skeptical at first about its potential impact. Slowly, Jane noticed a transformation. She started to see herself in a new light, focusing on her strengths and the positive aspects of her life rather than her perceived shortcomings. This shift helped her overcome negative self-perceptions, allowing her to build confidence in her abilities. Another example is Tim, who had always doubted his skills at work. He learned to appreciate his achievements and contributions through gratitude journaling, boosting his self-esteem and confidence. These stories illustrate the transformative power of gratitude, showing how it can elevate self-worth and foster personal growth.

Gratitude journaling can be a gratifying practice that enhances your self-worth and enriches your daily experiences. As you cultivate gratitude, you create a positive foundation supporting your mental and emotional well-being. This practice encourages you to celebrate the small victories in life, recognizing the beauty and abundance surrounding you. It is about acknowledging the good, even amid challenges, and allowing that recognition to fuel your sense of worthiness and joy. As you continue to explore gratitude journaling, remember that it is a personal journey that invites you to discover the richness of your life and the inherent value you hold within.

AFFIRMATION PRACTICES FOR PERSONAL GROWTH

Do you wake up each morning with a chorus of negative thoughts echoing in your mind, telling you what you cannot do or who you are not? This negativity can be relentless, impacting how you view yourself and your potential. That is where positive affirmations come into play. They serve as powerful tools in personal development, helping to challenge and reshape those deep-seated negative self-beliefs. You create a positive self-image that reflects your true potential by consistently affirming your worth and abilities. Affirmations can help resolve conflicting internal messages about self-worth when dealing with disorganized attachment patterns. They reinforce the belief that you are capable and deserving of growth and success, shifting your mindset from doubt to possibility.

Crafting effective affirmations requires thoughtful consideration. Begin using the present tense and positive language, as if what you affirm is already true. For instance, say, "I am confident and capable," rather than "I will be confident someday." This approach helps your mind accept these statements as reality, creating a sense of immediacy and certainty. Focus on specific goals or qualities that resonate deeply with you, ensuring that your affirmations align with your values and aspirations. This personalization makes the affirmations more meaningful and impactful, as they speak directly to your unique journey and desires.

The science behind affirmations supports their effectiveness. Research indicates that affirmations can influence neural pathways, promoting positive thinking and altering the brain's response to stress. When you repeat affirmations, you engage the brain's reward system, reinforcing positive beliefs and reducing the impact of negative ones. This neural reprogramming helps cultivate a more resilient and adaptable mindset, enhancing overall psychological well-being. By inserting affirmations into your daily routine, you can harness the brain's plasticity to foster growth and transformation, paving the way for a more empowered self.

Daily affirmations in your life can be simple yet transformative. Start with morning affirmation practices, setting aside a few minutes each day to recite your affirmations aloud or in your mind. It sets a positive tone for the day, grounding you in the beliefs that you wish to cultivate. Consider using affirmation cards, which you can place around your home or workspace as constant reminders of your intentions. These visual cues can reinforce your affirmations throughout the day, helping to keep your mindset aligned with your goals. As you fold these practices into your routine, you may notice a shift in how you perceive yourself and interact with the world, embracing opportunities for growth with confidence and clarity.

BUILDING AN INNER SUPPORT SYSTEM

Envision a world where you possess an unwavering sense of stability and support, no matter the external circumstances. This is the essence of an inner support system—a network of personal resources that bolsters your confidence and resilience. Developing self-reliance is the cornerstone of this system. It involves trusting your abilities and judgments and knowing that you have the strength to face challenges independently. This self-confidence acts as a buffer against the uncertainties of life, providing a sense of security that is not reliant on external validation. Reinforcing this system is the cultivation of inner resilience. It is the ability to adapt and recover from adversity, and it is fortified by a strong inner support system that can gracefully weather life's storms.

The benefits of a robust inner support system are manifold. Chief among them is increased self-trust. When you trust yourself, you navigate life's challenges with assurance, knowing you have the necessary tools to succeed. This trust fosters a sense of autonomy, allowing you to confidently make decisions, free from the paralyzing fear of making mistakes. Additionally, an inner support system equips you to self-soothe during times of stress. Instead of seeking external comfort, you can draw upon your internal resources to calm and center yourself. This self-soothing ability is invaluable in maintaining emotional equilibrium, helping you manage stress and anxiety effectively. For those with disorganized attachment histories, building an inner support system is crucial for developing the consistent internal presence that may have been missing in early relationships.

Creating and maintaining your inner support system begins with identifying your strengths and resources. Take some time to reflect on your abilities, talents, and past successes. What qualities have helped you overcome challenges? Perhaps it is your perseverance, creativity, or empathy. Recognize these strengths and use them as the foundation of your inner support system. Once you have identified your strengths, consider creating a personal mantra or support statement. This mantra should encapsulate your core values and beliefs, providing motivation and encouragement during difficult times. Repeat this mantra regularly to reinforce your inner support system, making it a central part of your self-care routine.

Consider Rachel, who found herself at a crossroads in her career. Faced with uncertainty, she relied on her inner support system to navigate the transition. Rachel confidently approached the situation by focusing on her strengths, such as her adaptability and problem-solving skills. Her mantra, "I am capable and resourceful," became a guiding light, helping her maintain composure and clarity. Similarly, David faced a challenging family situation that tested his emotional resilience. He strengthened his inner support system through meditation and self-reflection, allowing him to remain calm and composed. These stories illustrate the power of internal support, demonstrating how it can provide stability and strength in the face of adversity.

As you cultivate your inner support system, remember it is a dynamic and evolving structure. Like any other relationship, it requires regular attention and nurturing. Investing in your internal resources creates a bedrock of strength and resilience that empowers you to face life's challenges confidently and gracefully. This inner support system enhances your well-being and enriches your interactions with others, fostering more profound and meaningful connections.

In this chapter, we have explored various strategies to cultivate self-worth and self-compassion. As you build on these concepts, you will be better equipped to handle life's challenges. Next, we will examine how managing emotional closeness and vulnerability can further enhance relationships and personal growth.

CHAPTER 6

MANAGING EMOTIONAL CLOSENESS AND VULNERABILITY

Picture yourself standing before a window, the light streaming softly, illuminating the room with warmth. This moment is akin to emotional closeness in relationships—a gentle, illuminating presence that fosters connection and understanding. Emotional closeness is the heart of any meaningful relationship. It involves sharing personal thoughts and feelings, creating a bridge of understanding between individuals. When you share your inner world with someone, you invite them into your life in a way that builds a profound bond. This sharing is about speaking and engaging in meaningful conversations where both people feel heard and valued. These interactions become the threads that weave the fabric of your connection, each exchange strengthening the relational tapestry. As we have discussed, emotional closeness can feel simultaneously desired and threatening for those with disorganized attachment patterns. Understanding this paradox is crucial for developing healthier relationship dynamics.

UNDERSTANDING AND FOSTERING EMOTIONAL CLOSENESS

The benefits of emotional closeness are manifold. When two people connect on this level, trust naturally flourishes. In a world of uncertainty, having someone you can rely on is invaluable. This trust provides support and a safety net for life's challenges. But it is not just about leaning on each other in tough times. It is also about the joyous moments, the celebrations, and the shared laughter that make life beautiful. Greater empathy, a key ingredient in fostering emotional closeness, emerges from this connection, allowing you to understand your partner's perspective with clarity and compassion. As empathy deepens, so does relational satisfaction, as both feel seen and understood. This satisfaction is not fleeting; the deep contentment comes from knowing you are accepted and loved for who you are.

Yet, achieving emotional closeness is not without its challenges. Fear of rejection or judgment can act as a formidable barrier. You might hesitate to open up, worried that revealing your true self could lead to criticism or distancing. Past experiences of betrayal can also cast long shadows, making it difficult to trust again. These fears create walls that hinder intimacy, leaving you isolated even when surrounded by loved ones. It is a paradox of wanting closeness but fearing the vulnerability it requires. Understanding these barriers is crucial, allowing you to approach them with awareness and intention. Those working through disorganized attachment patterns, which can show as a fear of intimacy or a tendency to push people away, may find that emotional closeness triggers conflicting impulses to both seek and avoid intimacy.

Recognizing these patterns is the first step toward building more secure connections.

Intentional strategies can be employed to foster emotional closeness. One practical approach is to put aside dedicated time for deep conversations. It is easy to let meaningful dialogue fall by the wayside in our busy lives. By prioritizing these moments, you signal to your partner that they are essential and that their thoughts and feelings matter. This dedicated time creates a space free from distractions where you can explore each other's inner worlds. Again, another strategy is practicing active listening and empathy. It is a powerful way to enhance emotional closeness. This means not just hearing the words spoken but understanding the emotions behind them. It is being fully present, offering undivided attention, and responding empathetically. Doing so creates an environment where emotional closeness can thrive, nurtured by mutual understanding and respect.

Reflection Section: Cultivating Closeness

Take a moment to reflect on a recent conversation in which you felt emotionally close to someone. What exchange fostered that closeness? Consider how you can replicate these conditions in future interactions. Write down a list of actions or attitudes contributing to this connection. This reflection can guide you in nurturing emotional closeness in your relationships, helping you build more profound and meaningful connections.

TECHNIQUES TO EMBRACE VULNERABILITY

Vulnerability is the hidden strength in relationships, the quiet courage that builds deep, lasting connections. When you are vulnerable, you let go of the need for perfection. You open the door to authenticity by showing your true self and flaws. By sharing your weaknesses and fears, you invite others to do the same, fostering a space of mutual openness. It is in these shared imperfections that genuine connections form. Vulnerability allows you to be seen for who you are, not just the polished version you present to the world. This transparency can strengthen bonds, encouraging others to reciprocate with their truths and creating a foundation of trust and understanding.

Becoming comfortable with vulnerability is a journey that requires self-compassion. It is a practice of gradual self-disclosure in environments where you feel safe. Start small. Share a personal story or an emotion with someone you trust. Notice how it feels to open up and how the other person responds. Safe environments, like close friendships or supportive family gatherings, are ideal places to practice this. You can expand this practice to other areas as you become more comfortable. Alongside this, cultivate self-compassion. When you feel exposed or unsure, remind yourself that vulnerability is a strength, not a weakness. This self-compassion is a cushion, softening the edges of exposure and encouraging further openness. It is important to remember that self-compassion is not just a tool but a comforting companion in embracing vulnerability.

Vulnerability plays a pivotal role in resolving conflicts. Disagreements escalate because people hide their true feelings behind defensiveness or anger. By expressing emotions honestly, you can break down these barriers. Saying, "I felt hurt when you did that," rather than lashing out, invites understanding and resolution. This openness can transform conflict from a battleground into a space for growth and healing. Vulnerability fosters dialogue, allowing both people to express their feelings without fear of retribution. It requires courage but can lead to healthier, more constructive resolutions. When both people approach conflict with vulnerability, they pave the way for empathy, compassion, and a deeper connection. This power of empathy in resolving disputes can lead to a profound sense of growth and healing in your relationships.

Let us consider Esther, who found herself constantly clashing with her partner. Their arguments seemed to go in circles, leaving them both frustrated and disconnected. One day, Esther decided to try something different. Instead of pointing fingers, she shared her fears and insecurities, expressing how certain behaviors made her feel unloved. Her partner, taken aback by her candor, responded with his vulnerabilities. This exchange marked a turning point in their relationship. By embracing vulnerability, they discovered a new level of understanding and intimacy. Then there is Matthew, who struggled with being open about his mental health challenges. After years of silence, he confided in a close friend, revealing his struggles with anxiety. To his surprise, his friend responded with empathy and shared his experiences with similar issues. This moment of vulnerability deepened their friendship, creating a support system Matthew had not realized he needed. These stories illustrate the transformative power of vulnerability, showing that when you dare to be open, you invite others to connect with you profoundly and empower yourself.

PRACTICES FOR HEALTHY EMOTIONAL INTIMACY

As we have seen, emotional intimacy is the delicate art of deeply understanding another person while being understood yourself. It forms the core of profound relationships, fostering a solid framework of mutual respect and acceptance. When you comprehend your partner's inner world *and* your own, you create a bond that withstands time and change. Emotional intimacy transcends physical presence; it is about truly knowing each other and sharing life's vulnerabilities and joys. This deeper understanding allows you to anticipate each other's needs and respond with compassion and care, strengthening the relational fabric woven between you.

Consider incorporating practices that invite connection into your daily life to enhance emotional intimacy. One simple yet powerful exercise is sharing daily highs and lows with your partner. This practice encourages open dialogue about the day's events, fostering a deeper understanding of each other's experiences and emotions. Another effective method is creating rituals of connection. A weekly check-in, where you discuss your feelings, aspirations, and concerns, can be a dedicated space for intimacy to flourish. These rituals remind you to pause and focus on your relationship, reinforcing the importance of maintaining a strong emotional connection amid distractions.

However, maintaining emotional intimacy can be challenging, especially as routine and complacency set in over the years. Long-term relationships often fall into predictable patterns, where the initial excitement fades, and the daily grind takes over. This can lead to neglecting the emotional needs that once came so naturally. When life becomes a series of routines, intimacy can erode, leaving both partners feeling distant and disconnected. Recognizing this drift is crucial, allowing you to take proactive steps to reignite the emotional spark that initially drew you together.

To sustain emotional intimacy, regular expressions of appreciation and gratitude are vital. Taking the time to acknowledge and thank your partner for their efforts and qualities can breathe new life into your relationship. Simple acts like leaving a thoughtful note or verbally expressing gratitude can make your partner feel valued and loved. Additionally, engaging in new and shared experiences together can rekindle the connection. Whether trying out a new hobby, exploring a new place, or even taking a class together, these activities create shared memories and deepen your bond. They break the monotony and remind you of the joy of discovery that brought you together in the first place.

Incorporating these practices into your relationship nurtures the emotional intimacy that sustains lasting bonds. As you strive to understand and connect with your partner on a deeper level, you build a resilient and fulfilling relationship capable of weathering life's changes and challenges. This commitment to intimacy requires intention and effort, but the rewards—a profound connection and enduring love—are well worth it.

BALANCING CONNECTION AND INDEPENDENCE

Maintaining a balance between connection and independence is crucial in the tapestry of relationships. You want to preserve your individuality while building a close bond with your partner, but it can feel like walking a tightrope. Independence allows you to pursue personal interests and hobbies, giving you space to grow and explore. This freedom fuels your sense of self, ensuring you do not lose sight of who you are outside the relationship. Encouraging your partner's autonomy is equally essential. It is about supporting their need for personal space and respecting their pursuits. For those with disorganized attachment histories, finding this balance can be particularly challenging, as early experiences may have created confusion about appropriate boundaries and connections. But when both partners find space to flourish independently, they bring more to the relationship, enriching the connection with new experiences and growth.

Yet, achieving this balance is not without its challenges. The fear of losing yourself in a relationship is common. You might worry that merging too closely with your partner could lead to losing your identity. This fear can create an internal conflict, where the desire for connection clashes with the need for independence. Conversely, dependency on a partner for emotional fulfillment can stifle both people. When one person relies too heavily on the other for happiness or validation, it can lead to feelings of suffocation and imbalance. This dependency can erode the relationship's foundation, making it difficult to maintain a healthy dynamic. Recognizing these challenges is the first step toward finding a harmonious balance.

As discussed in an earlier chapter, consider setting boundaries for personal space and time to nurture independence and connection. Boundaries create a protective bubble where you can recharge and pursue individual interests without guilt. Express your intimate needs and expectations directly to your partner to ensure you understand and respect each other's boundaries. This transparency fosters trust and prevents misunderstandings, allowing the relationship to thrive without compromising personal freedom. Practicing open communication involves regular check-ins where you discuss what is working and what is not. These conversations provide an opportunity to adjust and realign, ensuring both partners feel valued and understood. You create a framework supporting individuality and togetherness by setting clear boundaries and maintaining an open dialogue.

Consider the story of Lily and Sam, a couple who balanced their independence with their deep connection. A passionate artist, Lily needed time alone to create, while Sam thrived on social interactions and adventures. They established a routine where Lily had dedicated studio time, and Sam enjoyed outings with friends. They also set aside time for shared activities, strengthening their connection. This arrangement allowed them to support each other's passions while nurturing their relationship. Another example is Eveline and Joshua, who found balance by pursuing separate hobbies. Eveline loved yoga, while Josh was an avid cyclist. They encouraged each other to follow these interests and often shared stories and insights from their experiences, enriching their bond with new perspectives. These couples demonstrate that with intentional effort, it is possible to maintain individuality while cultivating a deep, fulfilling connection.

NAVIGATING VULNERABILITY IN NEW RELATIONSHIPS

Starting a new relationship is often an exhilarating yet daunting experience. The thrill of discovery mingles with the trepidation of revealing yourself to another person. In these early stages, vulnerability can feel particularly challenging. The fear of being hurt or rejected looms large, casting shadows over moments of budding intimacy. You may wonder if your new partner will accept you as you are or if showing too much too soon might drive them away. This fear is natural, as new relationships often bring uncertainties that test our willingness to open up. Vulnerability, however, is not about baring your soul all at once; it is about gradually taking measured steps to build trust and openness. Those healing from disorganized attachment may find new relationships particularly challenging as they navigate between intense desires for connection and equally intense fears of vulnerability.

Share small, personal details with your new partner to navigate these waters. This might be a childhood memory, a hobby you enjoy, or an emotion you felt during your day. Observe how they respond to these disclosures. Are they interested? Do they reciprocate with their own stories? Their responses can offer meaningful insights into the potential for a deeper connection. This gradual self-revelation allows you to gauge their capacity for empathy and understanding without overwhelming either party. As trust builds, you can slowly increase the depth of your disclosures, fostering a safe environment where both of you feel comfortable being yourselves.

In the context of new relationships, trust is the bedrock upon which vulnerability rests. As we saw in Chapter 3, building trust is a gradual process that demands patience and consistency. Trust is earned through actions that demonstrate reliability and integrity. Consistent behavior, such as keeping promises and punctuality, reinforces the belief that your partner is dependable. As your relationship grows, these actions create a secure foundation, allowing you to feel safe in your vulnerability. As trust grows, so does the willingness to share more intimate thoughts and feelings. This mutual trust paves the way for a more profound emotional connection, transforming initial uncertainty into a lasting bond.

Consider the story of Arthur and Mia, who met through mutual friends. Initially, Arthur hesitated to share his passion for poetry, fearing it might be seen as frivolous. Encouraged by Mia's genuine interest in his hobbies, he started sharing his favorite poems. Mia responded with enthusiasm, sharing her love for literature. This exchange marked the beginning of a deeper connection. As their trust in each other solidified, Arthur and Mia opened up about more personal topics, such as family dynamics and aspirations. Their relationship blossomed as each disclosure brought them closer, proving that vulnerability can be a powerful catalyst for intimacy when embraced thoughtfully.

Similarly, consider Claire, who entered a new relationship cautiously after a previous heartbreak. She explored the idea of vulnerability by sharing her love for painting, something she had kept private for years. Her partner, Ben, reacted with curiosity, asking questions and suggesting they visit an art gallery together. Encouraged by his supportive response, Claire gradually shared more about her artistic journey, including her dreams and fears. With each shared story, their bond deepened, and Claire realized that being vulnerable did not weaken her; it enriched her connection with Ben. These narratives illustrate that embracing vulnerability, even in small doses, can lead to meaningful and lasting relationships.

CHAPTER 7
EFFECTIVE COMMUNICATION IN RELATIONSHIPS

IN THE ORCHESTRA OF HUMAN INTERACTION, COMMUNICATION ACTS AS the conductor, guiding the symphony of words, gestures, and emotions that connect us. Yet, amid the cacophony of modern life, our ability to genuinely listen often falls silent, drowned out by the relentless tempo of distractions and responsibilities. Imagine a conversation where the speaker's words drift into an abyss of inattentiveness—their meaning lost in the noise of unending notifications and mental clutter. This scenario is all too familiar in a world where our attention is a prized commodity, constantly sought after by the demands of daily life. As we have mentioned in other chapters up to this point, active listening offers a beacon of clarity in this fog of distraction, inviting us to engage with others on a deeper, more meaningful level. For those with disorganized attachment patterns, communication can feel particularly challenging as it may trigger conflicting impulses to both connect and withdraw. Understanding these patterns is crucial for developing more consistent and secure communication styles.

THE ART AND IMPORTANCE OF ACTIVE LISTENING

Active listening is much more than hearing words; it is the art of fully engaging with the speaker and focusing intently on their message and emotions. Unlike passive listening, where words merely pass through our consciousness, active listening requires deliberate attention and presence. It involves reflecting on what is being said, not just the words but the emotions and intent behind them. By paraphrasing or summarizing the speaker's message, you can demonstrate understanding and empathy, creating a space where the other person feels honestly heard. This practice enhances communication and fosters intimacy and trust, laying the foundation for stronger relationships. The emotional benefits of active listening are significant, making it a skill worth mastering.

Despite its importance, active listening is often hindered by various barriers. Distractions are among the most common obstacles, drawing our focus away from the speaker and onto other stimuli. Whether it is the ping of a smartphone or the mental checklist of tasks yet to be completed, these interruptions can sever the connection thread, leaving the speaker feeling undervalued and ignored. Multitasking further compounds this issue, as dividing attention between multiple activities diminishes our capacity to engage with any task fully. Prejudgments and assumptions also pose significant barriers, as preconceived notions about a person's intentions or abilities can color our perception of their words, leading to misunderstandings and conflicts. These assumptions act as filters, distorting the speaker's message and preventing genuine communication. However, active listening can help overcome these barriers, as it encourages us to focus on the speaker's message and emotions rather than our distractions or assumptions. Those healing from disorganized attachment may find active listening incredibly challenging, as past experiences may have created heightened sensitivity to verbal and non-verbal cues. Learning to distinguish between past triggers and present communication becomes essential.

Practical techniques can overcome these barriers and enhance active listening skills. One of the most effective methods is maintaining eye contact. It shows the speaker you are fully present and engaged. This simple act can convey a sense of respect and attentiveness, encouraging open and honest dialogue. Using verbal affirmations, such as "I understand" or "That makes sense," can reinforce your engagement, demonstrating that you are actively processing the speaker's message. These affirmations serve as verbal nods, acknowledging the speaker's thoughts and emotions and fostering a deep connection. Additionally, reflecting on the speaker's words through paraphrasing can clarify understanding and ensure that both parties are on the same page.

Consider the story of a team leader, Spencer, who transformed a work environment plagued by misunderstandings through the power of active listening. He created a culture of respect and understanding by encouraging open dialogue and practicing attentive listening during meetings. Team members felt valued and heard, leading to increased collaboration and productivity. Similarly, active listening can bridge the gap between friends or partners in personal relationships, strengthening bonds and resolving conflicts. The transformative power of active listening to resolve disputes can bring hope and optimism to any relationship. We can learn from a couple who began practicing active listening after years of miscommunication. By genuinely hearing each other's concerns and perspectives, they were able to address underlying issues and foster a more harmonious relationship.

Interactive Exercise: Active Listening Practice

Try this simple exercise to hone your active listening skills. Pair up with a friend or partner and set a five-minute timer. One person speaks about a topic of their choice while the other listens attentively. The listener should maintain eye contact, refrain from interrupting, and use verbal affirmations. After the person speaking finishes, the listener paraphrases what was said to confirm understanding. Switch roles and repeat. Reflect on how this exercise changes the dynamic of your conversation and the connection you feel with your partner.

CLEARLY EXPRESSING EMOTIONS

Imagine sitting down with someone you care about, eager to share a moment of vulnerability, only to find the words tangled in your throat. This is a familiar scene for many, where the unspoken emotions create a barrier, leaving both people feeling distant and misunderstood. The ability to express emotions is a cornerstone of trust and intimacy. When you articulate your feelings openly, you invite transparency into the interaction, paving the way for deeper connections. For those with disorganized attachment histories, expressing emotions clearly can feel particularly risky, as early experiences may have taught that emotional expression leads to unpredictable responses. Building a new framework for emotional expression becomes crucial. By reducing misunderstandings, you create an environment where both people feel safe to share their authentic selves, fostering a bond built on mutual respect and understanding—transparent emotional expression bridges two hearts in a dance of empathy and compassion, reassuring both people of their security in the relationship.

Consider employing strategies that clarify and own your feelings to articulate emotions effectively. One powerful method is using "I" statements, which allow you to express your emotions without casting blame. For instance, saying, "I feel hurt when plans change unexpectedly," focuses on your feelings rather than accusing the other person of wrongdoing. This approach encourages open dialogue and reduces defensiveness, making it easier for the other person to engage with your perspective. Additionally, distinguishing between thoughts and feelings is crucial. Often, what we perceive as emotions are judgments or assumptions in disguise. By separating these elements, you gain clarity and can communicate more authentically. For example, instead of saying, "I feel like you're ignoring me," consider stating, "I feel lonely when you don't respond."

Despite its importance, many struggle to express emotions clearly due to various challenges. A common hurdle is the fear of vulnerability, where sharing emotions feels like exposing a tender underbelly. This fear can come from past experiences where vulnerability led to hurt or rejection. As a result, we may suppress our emotions, choosing silence over the risk of being misunderstood. Another significant challenge is the lack of an emotional vocabulary. We often resort to vague expressions without words to describe complex feelings, leaving our emotions open to misinterpretation. This lack of precision can lead to frustration and conflict, as neither party fully understands the other's emotional landscape.

Engaging in specific exercises can be beneficial to navigate these challenges and enhance clarity in emotional communication. Emotion journaling offers a private space to explore and articulate your feelings. By regularly writing about your emotions, you become more attuned to their nuances and can identify patterns or triggers. This practice improves your emotional vocabulary and provides insights into your inner world, enabling you to communicate more precisely. Additionally, role-playing emotional conversations can be an effective way to practice expressing emotions in a safe environment. By simulating real-life scenarios with a trusted friend or therapist, you can experiment with different ways of articulating your feelings, receiving feedback, and refining your approach. This rehearsal can build confidence, making expressing emotions clearly in actual situations easier.

The journey of expressing emotions is not about achieving perfection but embracing authenticity. It is about finding the courage to share your inner world with another, knowing that doing so can deepen your connection. As you practice articulating your emotions, you create a space where you and your partner can engage in meaningful dialogue, navigating the complexities of your relationship with openness and grace. In this dance of communication, each step toward clarity and honesty strengthens your bond, enriching your relationship and fostering a love grounded in understanding and trust.

CONFLICT RESOLUTION STRATEGIES

In every relationship, conflict is as inevitable as the changing seasons. Yet, how we approach and resolve these disagreements can significantly influence the health of our connections. Conflict resolution is not merely about finding a middle ground but is a vital component that strengthens relationships. Addressing issues constructively enhances mutual understanding, ensuring everyone feels heard and respected. This approach prevents resentment from festering, which, if left unchecked, can erode the foundation of even the strongest bonds. Consider conflict an opportunity to deepen your relationship, explore different perspectives, and grow together. Those working through disorganized attachment patterns may find conflict particularly triggering, as it can simultaneously activate both fight and flight responses. Understanding these reactions helps in developing more balanced conflict resolution strategies.

Effective conflict resolution relies on strategies to navigate disagreements with empathy and clarity. Finding common ground and reaching compromises are pivotal techniques. They involve identifying shared values or goals that can serve as a foundation for agreement. When both people focus on these commonalities, it becomes easier to negotiate solutions that respect each person's needs. Also, establishing fair fighting rules can prevent conflicts from escalating into heated arguments. These rules might include agreeing to take breaks when emotions run high or committing to speak calmly and respectfully. These guidelines create a structured environment where issues can be addressed without fear of personal attacks.

Setting and timing play crucial roles in the success of conflict resolution. Discussing sensitive issues at the wrong time can lead to misunderstandings and heightened emotions. Choosing the right moment—when both people are calm and receptive— ensures the conversation is productive. Similarly, the setting can influence the outcome of a discussion. A neutral, comfortable environment can help both people feel safe to talk about their thoughts and emotions. Creating a space free from distractions is vital, where the focus remains on resolving the conflict. This careful consideration of timing and setting sets the stage for meaningful dialogue, allowing for the possibility of resolution and reconciliation.

Consider the story of Dustin and Louise, whose relationship faced turbulence due to differing priorities. Their arguments often spiraled into blame games, leaving both people frustrated and disconnected. However, they transformed their disagreements into collaborative discussions by implementing conflict resolution strategies. During one such dispute, Dustin suggested they list their shared goals, which revealed more commonalities than differences. They agreed to compromise, aligning their priorities to accommodate each other's needs. This shared exercise resolved their immediate conflict and strengthened their bond, reinforcing the importance of teamwork and empathy.

In another instance, Sam and Alex navigated a conflict regarding household responsibilities, which had become a source of tension. By agreeing to rules for fair fighting, they approached the issue calmly, each taking turns articulating their feelings without interruption. They chose a quiet evening at home to discuss their concerns, ensuring a relaxed setting that encouraged openness.

This thoughtful approach allowed them to express their frustrations without escalating into personal attacks. Through mutual understanding and compromise, Sam and Alex created a chore schedule that balanced their contributions, resolving the conflict amicably and enhancing their sense of partnership.

Resolving conflicts constructively requires patience, empathy, and a willingness to see beyond immediate disagreements. It is about recognizing that beneath the surface tension lies an opportunity for growth and understanding. By employing effective strategies, you can transform conflicts into moments of connection, reinforcing the bonds that hold your relationship together.

BUILDING EMOTIONAL INTELLIGENCE

Imagine being in a crowded room filled with chatter and overlapping conversations. Yet, somehow, your attention zeros in on one person's expression—a subtle brow furrow and a slight downturn of the lips. This skill to pick up on emotional cues, to not only recognize but also understand the emotions of others, is a vital part of emotional intelligence (EQ). Emotional intelligence is knowing and controlling our feelings and handling interpersonal relationships judiciously and empathetically. It enhances interactions by allowing us to navigate the emotional terrain of relationships with insight and sensitivity. Recognizing our emotions and those of others enables us to manage them effectively, paving the way for smoother communication and deeper connections.

At the center of emotional intelligence lies self-awareness and self-regulation (as discussed in Chapter 2). Self-awareness is recognizing your emotions and understanding how they affect your behavior and thoughts. It is about acknowledging your strengths and weaknesses without judgment. When you are aware of your emotional states, you can manage them more effectively. Self-regulation follows naturally, enabling you to control impulsive reactions and healthily manage emotions. This skill allows you to pause before reacting, choosing responses central to your values and goals. Together, these elements form the foundation of EQ, providing stability and control in the face of emotional challenges. Another critical component is empathy—the ability to understand and share the feelings of another. Empathy bridges the emotional gap between people, fostering connection and trust. Coupled with social skills, which involve managing relationships and building networks, empathy allows you to communicate more effectively and resolve conflicts gracefully.

Developing emotional intelligence is an ongoing process involving deliberate practice and reflection. Again, mindfulness is a powerful tool in this endeavor, as it enhances self-awareness by encouraging you to observe your feelings and thoughts non-judgmentally. Practicing mindfulness can help you be more attuned to your emotional states, allowing you to respond rather than react. Engaging in perspective-taking exercises further sharpens your EQ, challenging you to see situations from another's viewpoint. This practice deepens empathy and enriches your understanding of diverse perspectives, enabling more nuanced and compassionate interactions. Adding these strategies into your daily life can cultivate more emotional intelligence, leading to more harmonious and fulfilling relationships.

For those healing from disorganized attachment, developing emotional intelligence includes learning to trust their emotional experiences while building the capacity to regulate intense reactions that stem from early attachment wounds. Consider the story of Michelle, who navigated complex social dynamics at work with newfound ease after enhancing her emotional intelligence. Previously, office politics left her feeling overwhelmed and isolated. By focusing on self-awareness and practicing mindfulness, Michelle learned to identify her triggers and manage stress more effectively. Her improved self-regulation allowed her to approach challenging colleagues calmly and poised, transforming tense interactions into productive dialogues. Another tale is that of Joaquin, who struggled to connect with his partner on an emotional level. Through empathy-building exercises, he learned to listen and validate his partner's feelings, leading to stronger, more empathetic connections. These transformations demonstrate the profound impact of enhanced emotional intelligence on professional and personal relationships, creating a ripple effect of understanding and connection. Emotional intelligence is not a destination but a path that enriches every interaction, guiding you toward more profound, meaningful connections.

DEVELOPING EMPATHIC COMMUNICATION SKILLS

While those with disorganized attachment patterns may have developed a heightened sensitivity to other's emotions as a survival mechanism, learning to channel this sensitivity into healthy empathic communication requires practice and patience.

Empathic communication is the bridge that connects one heart to another, fostering a deep mutual respect and understanding that transcends mere words. Hearing someone, truly understanding them, and sharing their emotional experience. This communication transforms interactions by reducing conflict and enhancing cooperation, encouraging openness and vulnerability. Empathy allows partners to feel seen and valued in relationships, creating a haven where both can express themselves without fear of judgment. Empathic communication is about tuning into the person's emotional frequency, resonating with their feelings, and responding with genuine care. It builds trust, allowing the relationship to flourish through shared understanding and compassion.

Specific techniques can be employed to cultivate empathic communication to nurture empathy in interactions. Practicing active listening with empathy involves being fully present and attentive to the other person's words and emotions. It is about setting aside your thoughts and focusing entirely on the speaker, acknowledging their feelings and experiences. Validating others' emotions is another critical aspect. By affirming their feelings, you show that you understand and respect their emotional state, even if you do not necessarily agree with their perspective. This validation creates a sense of security and acceptance, encouraging open dialogue and reducing defensiveness. Empathy becomes a natural part of your communication style through these practices, enriching your relationships with depth and understanding.

However, developing empathic communication is not without its challenges. Personal biases and assumptions can be significant barriers, clouding your judgment and keeping you from fully engaging with the other person's experience. These biases often stem from past experiences or ingrained beliefs, influencing how you perceive and interpret others' emotions. Overcoming these barriers requires consciously setting aside preconceived notions and approaching each interaction with an open mind and heart. Emotional reactivity is another obstacle that can block empathy by triggering defensive responses. When emotions run high, it can be difficult to remain empathetic and objective. Managing your emotional reactions is crucial for maintaining empathy, allowing you to respond calmly and thoughtfully rather than impulsively.

Specific exercises can be highly beneficial for practicing and strengthening empathic communication. Reflective listening exercises are an excellent way to hone your empathic skills. In these exercises, you listen to someone express their thoughts and emotions, then reflect on what you have heard to ensure understanding. This practice strengthens your ability to tune into the speaker's emotional state and respond effectively. Storytelling and role-playing are also effective methods for building empathy. By stepping into someone else's shoes and experiencing their story firsthand, you gain a deeper understanding of their emotions and perspectives. These exercises encourage you to empathize with a wide range of experiences, broadening your capacity for compassion and connection.

I often reflect on a couple I know who regularly use storytelling to strengthen their empathic communication. They create a rich tapestry of shared understanding and empathy by sharing personal anecdotes and exploring each other's emotional landscapes. This practice allows them to navigate challenges gracefully and patiently as they have cultivated a deep reservoir of compassion and insight. Another example involves friends who, through reflective listening exercises, have learned to support each other with empathy and care. This skill has transformed their friendship, allowing them to communicate openly and honestly, free from the constraints of judgment and misunderstanding. Empathic communication is not just a skill but a way of being that enriches every interaction and deepens every connection.

In this chapter, we have explored various communication techniques that can transform relationships, from active listening and expressing emotions clearly to resolving conflicts constructively and building emotional intelligence. These skills improve communication and foster deeper connections and understanding. Developing these skills will make your relationships more fulfilling and resilient. In the next chapter, we will explore how to cultivate secure attachments, building on the foundation of effective communication to create lasting and meaningful connections.

CHAPTER 8
SECURE ATTACHMENT AND HEALTHY RELATIONSHIPS

IMAGINE A WORLD WHERE RELATIONSHIPS FLOW LIKE A HARMONIOUS dance, each partner moving gracefully and understanding. This equilibrium is the essence of secure attachment, where love is a partnership built on trust and mutual respect. A securely attached person approaches relationships with a sense of balance, seamlessly integrating independence with the joys of connection. They walk through life with a harmonious rhythm, assured that they are worthy of love and capable of giving it. In such relationships, there is no need for pretense or games; authenticity and empathy take center stage, creating a stable foundation that weathers life's storms. For those healing from disorganized attachment, the journey toward secure attachment requires understanding that seemingly contradictory needs for closeness and distance are normal responses to early experiences.

UNDERSTANDING SECURE ATTACHMENTS

Secure attachment stands apart from other styles due to its core attributes. At its heart is the confidence in relationships that stems from a deep-seated belief in our value and the trustworthiness of others. This confidence allows us to engage fully with those around us, knowing that our worth does not hinge on the approval of others. This assuredness fosters resilience, enabling us to approach conflicts with calm and clarity. Securely attached individuals also master the art of balancing independence and interdependence. They understand the importance of maintaining their own identities while cherishing the connections they form. This equilibrium ensures they can pursue personal goals without fear of losing themselves in relationships, making room for personal growth and meaningful connection.

The emotional benefits of secure attachment weave a tapestry of stability and well-being. Reduced anxiety and fear of abandonment are prominent, as secure individuals trust in the strength of their relationships and have faith in their ability to navigate challenges. This emotional stability creates a sense of peace, allowing them to engage with others from a place of authenticity rather than fear. Their confidence in the resilience of their relationships reduces the need for excessive reassurance, freeing them to focus on the joy and fulfillment that connections bring. This foundation of trust and security enhances their well-being, providing a steady anchor in an unpredictable world. While those with disorganized attachment histories may initially find secure attachment traits foreign or frightening, these patterns can be learned through consistent, supportive relationships.

Behavioral indicators of secure attachment are transparent and observable. Effective communication is a cornerstone, as securely attached individuals prioritize open dialogue and active listening. They engage in conversations with empathy and respect, ensuring everyone feels heard and valued. Conflict resolution is approached with patience and understanding, as they seek to address differences constructively rather than defensively. This communication skill fosters an environment where issues can be resolved without resentment. Secure individuals are also willing to seek and offer support, understanding that relationships thrive on reciprocity. They know when to lean on others and when to be a source of strength, creating a dynamic of mutual empowerment.

Consider the scenario of a couple discussing their plans. Both partners approach the conversation with mutual respect, eager to understand each other's dreams and aspirations. They listen actively, offering encouragement and support as they explore possibilities together. Their dialogue is characterized by honesty and openness, free from the fear of judgment or rejection. In another example, friends supporting each other through life changes demonstrate secure attachment. Whether a career transition or a personal milestone, they stand by each other, offering reassurance and understanding. Their relationship is a safe space where they can express vulnerability and receive unwavering support.

Reflection Section: Identifying Secure Attachment in Your Life

Reflect on your relationships and consider moments where you felt secure and grounded. Write about the qualities that contributed to this sense of security and how you can nurture these traits further. Consider how you communicate, resolve conflicts, and offer support. This reflection can help you identify areas where secure attachment thrives and where it may need nurturing.

STEPS TO DEVELOP SECURE ATTACHMENT

Developing a secure attachment begins with understanding your personal attachment style. Recognizing whether you lean toward anxious, avoidant, or disorganized patterns can offer valuable insights into how you approach relationships. This self-awareness is the key to identifying behaviors that may hinder connection and working toward cultivating secure attachment traits. It is like holding a map of your emotional landscape, helping you navigate toward healthier interactions. Identifying patterns may reveal seemingly contradictory behaviors for those with disorganized attachment—both pursuing and avoiding closeness. For instance, you might find yourself craving intimacy but feeling overwhelmed when it becomes too intense. Understanding these patterns is crucial for transformation. Begin by reflecting on past relationships and noting recurring patterns. Ask yourself, "Do I often feel anxious about your partner's commitment? Do I tend to withdraw when intimacy deepens?" Understanding these tendencies is the first step toward a more secure attachment style.

As pointed out, setting and respecting personal boundaries is crucial once you have identified your attachment style. Boundaries are the invisible lines that protect your emotional and mental space, ensuring that your needs and values are honored.

They create a sense of safety and autonomy, allowing you to engage in relationships without losing yourself. Start by defining what feels comfortable for you in a relationship and communicate these boundaries to others. For instance, you might set a boundary around the amount of time you need for yourself each day or the level of emotional support you can provide without feeling overwhelmed. Respecting your boundaries reinforces self-worth, and respecting others' boundaries fosters trust and mutual respect. This practice lays the groundwork for secure, balanced relationships where both people feel valued and understood.

Again, self-awareness plays a pivotal role in this transformative process. Through self-reflection, you can recognize and transform attachment patterns that no longer serve you. Journaling is a powerful tool in this endeavor. You gain insights into triggers and habitual reactions by tracking your emotional responses. Writing down your feelings and thoughts lets you process emotions constructively, creating a space for growth and change. This practice enhances self-awareness and fosters emotional regulation, as well as managing and healthily responding to your feelings. It helps you react to situations more calmly and clearly. As you become more attuned to your internal landscape, you can make conscious choices that align with secure attachment behaviors.

To reinforce secure attachment traits, engage in practical exercises encouraging growth. Role-playing can be effective in practicing assertiveness. You can rehearse responses that honor your boundaries and needs by simulating challenging interactions. This practice builds confidence and prepares you for real-life situations. It enables you to communicate effectively and assertively. Also, mindfulness exercises can enhance emotional regulation, allowing you to navigate emotions easily. Deep breathing or meditation cultivates a sense of presence and calm, reducing reactivity and fostering emotional balance. These exercises equip you with the skills to approach relationships from a place of security and self-assurance.

Consider the story of Alisha, who once struggled with fears of vulnerability. She often felt exposed when opening up to others, fearing judgment or rejection. Through therapy and self-reflection, Alisha began to understand her anxious attachment style. She started journaling daily, which helped her identify fear and avoidance patterns. Over weeks and months, Alisha practiced role-playing with a friend, learning to assert her needs and express her feelings without anxiety. By consistently applying these strategies, she noticed a shift in her interactions. Her relationships became more fulfilling, characterized by trust and open communication. Alisha's journey illustrates how understanding and transforming attachment patterns can lead to a secure attachment style.

In another example, consider John, who faced difficulties with trust. His avoidant attachment style led him to withdraw emotionally, fearing dependency on others. Through mindfulness practices, John learned to stay present with his emotions rather than shutting down. He embraced exercises that encouraged openness, gradually building trust through consistent actions. John became more comfortable with intimacy by practicing assertiveness and respecting personal boundaries. His relationships became more supportive and stable as he learned to trust himself and others. John's story highlights the transformative power of cultivating secure attachment traits through intentional effort and practice.

BUILDING A SECURE BASE IN RELATIONSHIPS

In any relationship, the concept of a secure base holds immense significance. The emotional foundation provides safety and support, allowing us to explore the world confidently and grow personally. Imagine a tree with deep roots, anchoring it firmly while its branches stretch out freely. This secure base acts similarly, offering stability that encourages us to go beyond our comfort zones, ensuring they have a reliable place to return to. Emotional safety within a secure base means we feel accepted and valued, free to express ourselves without fear of judgment or rejection. This creates an environment where vulnerability is welcomed and authentic connections can thrive. Building a secure base is particularly important for those with disorganized attachment, as it provides the consistency and safety needed to develop new relationship patterns.

Creating a secure base requires intention and effort but is achievable through practical strategies. Maintaining open and honest communication is fundamental. This involves sharing thoughts and feelings transparently, fostering trust and understanding. When we communicate openly, we invite our partners into our inner world, allowing for deeper connections. Additionally, offering consistent reassurance and validation is crucial. This means acknowledging and affirming each other's emotions and experiences, reinforcing the idea that each person is valued and understood. Consistent reassurance helps to dispel doubts and insecurities, creating a nurturing environment where both people feel supported.

As discussed, mutual trust and respect are the cornerstones of a secure base. Trust-building activities, such as setting shared goals, engaging in cooperative tasks, or spending quality time together, can play a pivotal part in strengthening these elements. Through these experiences, we learn to rely on each other, deepening our bond and reinforcing trust. Respect is equally vital, ensuring that each person's boundaries and autonomy are honored. A secure base is constructed by upholding these values, providing a strong foundation for healthy and fulfilling relationships.

Consider a mentor-mentee relationship where growth is fostered through a secure base. The mentor provides guidance and support, encouraging the mentees to explore new opportunities and challenge themselves. This dynamic allows the mentee to take risks, knowing they have a real source of wisdom and encouragement to fall back on. Similarly, in family dynamics, a secure base can support individual autonomy. Family members provide a safety net, offering love and acceptance that empowers us to pursue our passions and make independent decisions. This support nurtures self-confidence and fosters a sense of belonging, reinforcing the secure base that underpins familial relationships.

In friendships, a secure base might manifest through unwavering support during life changes. Friends offer a listening ear, providing comfort and encouragement as one navigates transitions. This consistent presence instills a sense of security, knowing someone is there to lean on when needed. In romantic relationships, a secure base is evident in partners who champion each other's dreams. They celebrate successes and provide solace during setbacks, ensuring the A relationship is a sanctuary of support and understanding. Mutual encouragement nurtures growth and resilience, allowing each person to thrive individually and together.

A secure base is more than just a concept; it is a dynamic and evolving aspect of relationships. It requires active participation from everyone. We can cultivate a secure base that enriches relationships by prioritizing communication, reassurance, trust, and respect. This foundation allows for exploration, growth, and the joy of authentic connection, creating a relational environment where we are free to be our true selves.

TRANSFORMING RELATIONSHIP DYNAMICS

Changing the dynamics of a relationship often begins with recognizing and addressing negative behaviors that have become habitual. These behaviors might include patterns of communication that lead to misunderstandings or actions that inadvertently hurt one another. It is about becoming aware of these tendencies and consciously trying to change them. Encouraging positive communication habits is crucial. This means actively listening, speaking with empathy, and being open to feedback. It creates a space where both people feel safe to discuss their feelings and thoughts without fear of criticism or dismissal. This transformation does not happen quickly; it requires dedication and a willingness to shift old patterns into healthier ones.

Implementing regular check-ins can be incredibly practical in fostering change in relationship dynamics. These are dedicated times when you and your partner can openly discuss the state of your relationship. It is a chance to address concerns, celebrate successes, and plan for the future. Check-ins help prevent issues from festering and becoming more significant problems. They also reinforce the bond between partners by showing commitment to the relationship's health. During these conversations, it is vital to approach topics with curiosity rather than judgment. This openness encourages honest dialogue and mutual understanding, laying the groundwork for lasting change.

Patience and persistence are vital in this process. Relationship dynamics that have been in place for years will not change overnight. Unlearning old habits and building new ones takes time. Patience allows for the inevitable mistakes and setbacks, while persistence ensures you keep moving forward. Both partners must commit to the long-term goal of a healthier relationship. This means being willing to try again despite failures and remaining hopeful that change is possible. Over a year, these efforts can lead to profound shifts in how you relate to one another, resulting in a more fulfilling and harmonious partnership.

Consider the story of Liz and Cal, a couple in constant conflict. They realized that their arguments were fueled by miscommunication and unaddressed grievances. By committing to regular check-ins, they better understood each other's perspectives. They practiced active listening and learned to express their needs without blame. Within a year, their conflicts became less frequent and more constructive. They discovered a newfound understanding and respect for each other, strengthening their relationship. Similarly, friends like Cynthia and Carla, who experienced a betrayal, rebuilt their trust by addressing the hurt openly. They committed to transparency and consistency, restoring their friendship to mutual support and care.

REPAIRING ATTACHMENT RUPTURES

Attachment ruptures—moments when the emotional connection is temporarily broken—are inevitable in any relationship. For those healing from disorganized attachment, these ruptures can feel particularly threatening, often triggering intense fears of abandonment or rejection. Understanding that ruptures are opportunities for repair and strengthening bonds, rather than signs of relationship failure, is crucial for building secure attachments.

The repair process has several key steps:

1. Acknowledging the rupture without shame or blame
2. Creating space for both partners to express their emotional experience
3. Taking responsibility for our role in the disconnection
4. Working together to understand triggers and patterns
5. Developing specific strategies to prevent similar ruptures
6. Rebuilding emotional connection through small, consistent actions

Consider Maria and James, who experienced a rupture when James withdrew during a conflict. Instead of interpreting his withdrawal as rejection, Maria recognized it as a trauma response. They worked together to understand their triggers and developed a "time-in" protocol—a structured way to maintain connection even when needing space. This approach transformed their ruptures from threats to opportunities for deeper understanding.

MAINTAINING SECURE ATTACHMENTS AS PARTNERS

Maintaining secure attachments requires continuous effort and intention in the ever-evolving landscape of relationships. It is easy to assume that once a secure attachment is formed, it will remain strong without further nurturing. However, like a garden that flourishes with regular care, relationships thrive when they are consistently tended to. Sustaining secure attachments involves continuously nurturing emotional intimacy, ensuring the bonds of connection remain vibrant and resilient. This means actively engaging with your partner, sharing experiences, and staying attuned to each other's emotional needs. When both partners invest in maintaining this closeness, they create a space where love and understanding can grow unimpeded by neglect or complacency.

Relationships inevitably face challenges that can disrupt even the most secure attachments. Life transitions, such as moving to a new city or changing jobs, can introduce stress and uncertainty. These changes can alter the dynamics of a relationship, testing its strength and adaptability. During these times, secure attachments may be threatened by the anxiety of the unknown or the demands of new responsibilities. It is crucial to acknowledge these potential obstacles, and addressing them with openness and empathy is just as important. By recognizing the impact of these transitions, couples can work together to navigate them, ensuring that their connection remains strong despite external pressures. This forward-thinking approach helps reduce the risk of drifting apart during periods of change.

There are practical strategies that couples can employ to reinforce secure attachments. Regular relationship check-ins provide an opportunity to connect deeply and address any concerns before they escalate. These check-ins are moments to express gratitude, share feelings, and discuss future aspirations. They allow partners to align their goals and reaffirm their commitment to one another. Also, engaging in shared activities and experiences can strengthen the bond between partners. Whether it is a weekend getaway, a cooking class, or a walk in the park, these shared moments create cherished memories and deepen the emotional connection. By prioritizing quality time together, couples can fortify their attachment, making it more resilient to external stressors.

Consider the story of Phyllis and Jack, a couple celebrating decades of mutual support and love. Over the years, they have faced numerous challenges, including career changes and family responsibilities. Yet, they have remained steadfast in their commitment to each other, regularly setting aside time for one another. Their relationship check-ins have become a cherished ritual, allowing them to maintain a deep understanding of each other's needs and desires. Similarly, lifelong friends Stella and Bob have weathered various life stages together. They have supported each other through personal and professional milestones, always trying to stay connected despite geographical distances. Their friendship is a testament to the power of consistency and shared experiences in maintaining secure attachments.

Setting the Pace in New Relationships

Beyond the initial foundations discussed, pacing in relationships requires a delicate balance of self-awareness and communication. Consider Marcus's experience: He previously rushed into relationships only to feel overwhelmed and withdrawn. After working on his attachment patterns, he developed a personal "relationship speedometer"—checking in with himself regularly about his comfort levels with emotional and physical intimacy.

Key aspects of healthy pacing include the following:

- Creating space for individual growth while building connection
- Discussing expectations about time spent together
- Maintaining outside friendships and interests
- Gradually increasing emotional vulnerability
- Respecting each person's need for space and processing time

For example, Sally and Ken agreed to have "pace-setting conversations" every few weeks, openly discussing their comfort levels with the relationship's progression. This helped them navigate differences in their preferred speeds of emotional intimacy and prevented either partner from feeling pressured or held back.

Building Trust Gradually

Trust-building resembles constructing a bridge —it requires careful attention to foundation, regular maintenance, and patience. Steve and Mel demonstrated this by starting with small trust exercises: sharing minor vulnerabilities and observing how others handled them before moving to more profound disclosures.

Practical trust-building steps might include the following:

- Making and keeping small commitments consistently
- Being transparent about availability and boundaries
- Acknowledging and repairing minor ruptures promptly
- Demonstrating reliability in day-to-day interactions
- Respecting stated limits and preferences

Consider developing a "trust portfolio" by documenting instances where trust was honored. This will help you maintain perspective during challenging times and create a concrete reference point for the relationship's reliability and growth.

SECURE ATTACHMENT IN FAMILY RELATIONSHIPS

Family relationships often serve as the blueprint for our attachment styles, yet they also offer opportunities for healing and growth. Picture a family dinner where tension simmers beneath polite conversation. The patterns you develop in childhood may still influence these interactions, but understanding them provides a chance for transformation. Through conscious effort and practice, you can begin to create more secure bonds with family members, even if past relationships were marked by insecurity or trauma.

Creating secure attachments within families requires intentional effort and understanding, particularly when transforming established patterns. The Chen family exemplifies this transformation, having shifted from anxiety-driven interactions to more secure connections through conscious effort and professional guidance.

Secure family attachment manifests through consistent emotional availability and clear communication about needs and boundaries. It requires a delicate balance between respecting individual autonomy and maintaining strong connections. Regularly repairing ruptures and celebrating individual differences become cornerstones of family security. These elements create a foundation where family members feel safe expressing themselves authentically.

The Martinez family demonstrates how to implement these principles through structured connection points. They established daily one-on-one time with each child, creating spaces for undivided attention and emotional attunement. Weekly family meetings provide forums for open discussion, while monthly individual parent-child outings strengthen specific relationships. Quarterly family reviews help track progress and set new goals for a deeper connection.

Families must acknowledge inherited patterns without assigning blame when addressing multigenerational attachment patterns. This process involves creating new family rituals that support security and developing a shared language for emotional needs. Regular opportunities for repair and celebrating small shifts toward security become essential. These steps help break negative cycles while building stronger family bonds.

Extended family relationships add another layer of complexity to attachment dynamics. Success requires setting clear boundaries while maintaining meaningful connections. Families must learn to respect different attachment styles while creating safe spaces for difficult conversations. Establishing protocols for managing conflicts helps navigate challenging situations while building new traditions can support security across the extended family network.

NAVIGATING WORKPLACE ATTACHMENTS

Professional relationships significantly impact our daily well-being and often mirror our attachment patterns. Understanding and managing workplace attachments can enhance both professional success and personal growth. These relationships require careful attention to boundaries and communication while supporting professional development.

Secure leadership demonstrates consistent and clear communication while maintaining appropriate professional boundaries. Effective leaders recognize team members' needs while balancing autonomy and support. Regular feedback and acknowledgment foster a workplace where team members feel safe taking risks and growing professionally.

Holly's transformation of her department illustrates attachment-aware leadership in action. She established consistent communication channels with each team member through regular one-on-one check-ins. Clear expectations and structured feedback processes created predictability, while support for professional growth demonstrated investment in team development. Her attention to work-life boundaries helped maintain appropriate professional relationships.

Managing professional boundaries requires careful attention to role definition and appropriate emotional distance without withdrawal. This balance includes thoughtful sharing of personal information and maintaining consistent professional boundaries. Regularly reviewing professional relationships helps ensure they remain healthy and productive.

Authority figure relationships often trigger attachment patterns in our personal lives. Successfully managing these relationships involves balancing needs for autonomy and guidance while handling feedback and evaluation. Power dynamics require careful navigation, and building professional trust takes time and consistency.

Peer relationships in the workplace present unique challenges in maintaining appropriate closeness while managing competitive elements. Supporting colleague growth while handling workplace conflicts requires emotional intelligence and clear boundaries. Building collaborative relationships strengthens team effectiveness and our professional development.

Remote work has also added new dimensions to workplace attachment. Building connections through digital means requires intentional effort to maintain a presence without physical proximity. Creating virtual team cohesion while managing digital boundaries has become increasingly important. Supporting remote team attachment often requires new approaches to communication and connection.

Success in workplace attachments ultimately depends on self-awareness of attachment patterns and maintaining professional boundaries. Regular relationship assessment and ongoing professional development support healthy workplace connections. Understanding these dynamics helps create workplace environments that support individual and organizational growth while maintaining appropriate professional distance.

As this chapter draws to a close, it is clear that secure attachments are not static; they are dynamic, living entities that require ongoing care and attention. By continuously nurturing these connections, we can ensure that our relationships remain healthy and fulfilling. The effort invested in maintaining secure attachments pays dividends in the form of emotional stability, trust, and enduring love. As you reflect on these insights, consider how to apply them to cultivate lasting connections in your life. In the next chapter, we will explore the broader implications of secure attachments and how they influence personal growth and fulfillment, offering a deeper understanding of relationships' role in our lives.

CHAPTER 9

INTEGRATING PERSONAL GROWTH INTO DAILY LIFE

Envision awakening each day with a clear sense of direction, where every moment presents an opportunity to draw nearer to your aspirations. The seemingly insignificant daily habits can silently revolutionize your life over time. Consider the British Cycling Team, whose remarkable achievements were not the result of drastic changes but the refinement of their daily routines. This chapter delves into how you can implement similar strategies to your personal growth, redefining success as a steady accumulation of progress rather than sporadic leaps.

CREATING DAILY HABITS FOR PERSONAL GROWTH

The power of daily habits is the backbone of long-term success that can transform your aspirations into achievable realities. Starting your day with a purposeful morning routine can create an uplifting atmosphere that carries through and resonates throughout the hours ahead. Consider the difference between waking up to a cluttered mind versus beginning with a clear plan. A morning ritual, such as spending a few minutes setting intentions or engaging in light exercise, can sharpen your focus and boost productivity. These practices anchor you, offering a sense of control and readiness for whatever the day holds. At the other end of the day, evening reflections serve as a moment of pause, allowing you to assess daily progress and recalibrate as needed. By taking stock of what went well and identifying areas for improvement, you cultivate a growth mindset that keeps you motivated and aligned with your goals. These reflections are not about self-criticism but about fostering self-awareness and celebrating small wins.

Incorporating practical daily habits can significantly support your personal development journey. For instance, reading a chapter of a self-development book each day expands your knowledge and inspires new ideas and perspectives. This habit can be a source of daily motivation, prompting you to think differently and consider new approaches to challenges. Similarly, setting daily intentions can focus your energy and efforts toward specific goals. By starting each day with a clear intention, you direct your actions with purpose, transforming vague aspirations into concrete achievements. These habits, though simple, have the potential to create a powerful momentum that catapults you forward. Consistency matters more than perfection when establishing habits to overcome past emotional attachment wounds. Small, regular steps toward security build new neural pathways.

Consider the concept of habit stacking, a powerful tool that can further enhance your growth efforts. This involves linking new habits to established routines, making them easier to adopt and maintain. For instance, you can integrate a gratitude practice with your morning coffee ritual. As you savor the warmth of your drink, take a moment to reflect on three things you are grateful for. This practice enriches your morning routine and cultivates a mindset of appreciation that can positively influence your day. Similarly, pairing daily walks with listening to motivational podcasts is another effective strategy. Combining physical activity with learning maximizes the benefits of simultaneously nurturing your mind and body. Habit stacking leverages the power of current routines to support the adoption of new, beneficial behaviors, increasing the likelihood of long-term success. It is a tool that empowers you to take control of your growth journey.

Maintaining consistency in daily habits can be challenging, but it is essential for sustained growth. Using habit trackers can provide visual motivation by allowing you to monitor your progress. Each tick on the tracker represents a step forward, offering tangible evidence of your commitment and effort. This visual record can inspire persistence, especially when progress feels slow or stagnant. Celebrating small wins is another strategy to reinforce habit formation. Acknowledge and reward yourself for each milestone, no matter how minor it may seem. These celebrations create positive associations with your efforts, encouraging you to continue and build on your successes. They are the fuel that keeps your motivation burning bright.

Interactive Element: Creating Your Daily Habit Tracker

Design a simple habit tracker to monitor your progress. List your daily habits and mark each day you complete them. Reflect on patterns or challenges you notice, and adjust your approach as needed. Use this tool to celebrate your achievements and stay motivated on your growth journey.

CONTINUOUS SELF-REFLECTION PRACTICES

Imagine standing in front of a mirror, reflecting your outward appearance and the intricate tapestry of your thoughts, emotions, and aspirations. This is the essence of self-reflection—a powerful tool that fosters growth by shining a light on your inner world. Regular self-reflection encourages a deeper understanding of yourself, guiding you toward personal development. Weekly journaling allows for capturing insights and reflections, providing a written record of your thoughts and feelings. This practice enables you to observe patterns, notice shifts in perspective, and gain clarity on issues that might have seemed daunting. Self-reflection helps identify secure and insecure attachment patterns, allowing for conscious relationship choices. By dedicating time each week to journaling, you create a habit of introspection, turning the act of writing into a ritual that nurtures self-awareness and encourages emotional release.

Monthly reviews take self-reflection a step further, offering an opportunity to reassess your goals and progress. This practice invites you to step back and view your life from a broader perspective, evaluating where you stand concerning your aspirations. By reviewing the past month, you can acknowledge accomplishments, recognize areas for growth, and refine your goals as needed. This continuous reflection and adjustment cycle helps align your goals with your evolving values and priorities. It becomes a compass that guides your life's direction, keeping you on track and motivated to pursue growth with intention and purpose. Through these structured moments of reflection, you cultivate a mindset of continuous improvement, transforming challenges into opportunities for learning and development.

To enhance your self-reflection practices, consider employing SWOT analysis tools. Often used in business, this technique can be adapted to explore your "strengths, weaknesses, opportunities, and threats." You can use your strengths to navigate challenges and seize growth opportunities by identifying them. Acknowledging weaknesses allows for targeted improvement, while recognizing external opportunities and threats can inform your decision-making. Reflective prompts also serve as a valuable aid in self-reflection, guiding you to explore emotions and thoughts profoundly and honestly. These prompts might include questions like, "What am I grateful for today?" or "What challenges have I overcome this week?" By responding to such questions, you delve into your inner experiences, gaining insights that might otherwise remain hidden.

Self-reflection plays a vital role in setting goals and achievement. It informs and refines your goals, ensuring they are grounded in reality and aligned with your authentic self. Through reflection, you gain clarity on what truly matters to you, allowing you to set goals that resonate with your core values. This clarity enhances your motivation and increases the likelihood of achieving your objectives. Reflecting on your progress, you may find that some goals need adjustment based on personal insights. This flexibility is key to maintaining momentum and ensuring that your path to growth remains dynamic and responsive to change. Regularly reassessing your goals creates a feedback loop that supports sustained personal development, turning aspirations into actionable steps toward fulfillment.

To deepen your self-reflection practices, consider engaging in exercises that encourage introspection and understanding. Meditation focused on self-inquiry is one such practice that invites you to explore your inner world with curiosity and openness. Through meditation, you quiet the mind and create space for insights to emerge, allowing you to connect with your true self. This practice fosters a sense of peace and acceptance, facilitating a deeper understanding of your thoughts, emotions, and desires. Creative expression, such as drawing or painting, offers another avenue for self-reflection. By engaging in artistic activities, you tap into your subconscious mind, giving form to thoughts and feelings that might not be easy to articulate verbally. This expression lets you explore your inner landscape non-linearly, revealing new perspectives and insights.

These practices make self-reflection a powerful ally in your growth journey. It encourages you to look within, delve into your inner self, and discover profound wisdom. As you continuously self-reflect, you develop a deeper understanding of yourself, strengthening your foundation for growth and transformation. This process is not about achieving perfection but embracing the fullness of who you are, with all your strengths and vulnerabilities. Through self-reflection, you cultivate a relationship with yourself that is grounded in authenticity, compassion, and a commitment to lifelong learning.

THE ROLE OF GRATITUDE IN PERSONAL DEVELOPMENT

Imagine a day when you pause amid the chaos to give thanks for a stranger's smile, the warmth of the sun on your face, or the quiet comfort of your home. These small acts of gratitude can profoundly affect your mindset, turning ordinary moments into sources of joy and contentment. Gratitude is more than just a word of "thanks"; it is a mindset that fosters resilience and optimism. When you consciously focus on what you have rather than what you lack, it shifts your perspective from scarcity to abundance, enhancing your well-being and satisfaction. This focus on the positive can build mental resilience, enabling you to face challenges with a stronger, more optimistic outlook.

Embracing gratitude can increase resilience, helping you bounce back from adversity more robustly. When faced with difficulties, gratitude allows you to see beyond the immediate pain and recognize the silver linings. It shifts attention from what is wrong to what is right, fostering a sense of optimism that fuels perseverance. This shift enhances personal satisfaction and helps maintain a balanced emotional state. Acknowledging the good in your life can serve as an anchor in turbulent times, providing a sense of stability and hope. By regularly practicing gratitude, you cultivate a mindset that sees challenges as opportunities for growth instead of insurmountable obstacles.

To cultivate gratitude, consider maintaining a daily gratitude journal. This practice entails dedicating a few moments daily to writing down things you appreciate. It could be as small as enjoying a tasty meal or having a heartfelt conversation with a friend. Over time, this habit helps train your mind to recognize and hone in on the positive aspects of daily life, fostering a mindset that nurtures personal growth. Writing thank-you notes is another powerful way to express appreciation. By taking the time to acknowledge the kindness of others, you not only strengthen your connections but also reinforce your gratitude mindset. These practices can transform your outlook, making gratitude a natural part of your daily life.

The transformative power of gratitude is its ability to shift negative thought patterns. When you approach life with gratitude, you begin to reframe challenges as opportunities for growth. Instead of viewing obstacles as setbacks, you see them as stepping stones toward personal development. This perspective can diminish frustration and helplessness, empowering you to take proactive steps toward your goals. Gratitude encourages you to adopt a growth mindset, where you perceive difficulties as chances to learn and evolve. This change in outlook can enhance resilience and promote a more flexible approach to life's challenges.

Consider the story of Carl, who faced unexpected job loss. Initially overwhelmed by anxiety and uncertainty, Carl decided to focus on gratitude. Each day, he wrote down three things he appreciated, from the support of his family to the opportunity to explore new career paths. This practice helped him remain optimistic and open to possibilities, eventually leading him to a fulfilling new position. In another example, the Johnson family began a weekly tradition of sharing what they were grateful for. This simple ritual brought them closer, fostering stronger bonds and a shared appreciation. These stories illustrate how gratitude can lead to positive transformations, turning adversity into a catalyst for growth and connection.

Gratitude is not just an emotion but a powerful tool for personal development, reshaping how you interact with the world. By incorporating gratitude into your daily life, you enhance your resilience, foster deeper connections, and cultivate a mindset of abundance. This chapter has explored various aspects of personal growth, from building daily habits to practicing mindfulness and self-reflection. As you continue integrating these practices into your life, remember that gratitude can guide your journey and pave the way for lasting fulfillment.

MANAGING SETBACKS AND RELAPSES

Healing is not linear—it is a journey of progress and occasional steps backward. Picture yourself implementing new communication strategies in a relationship when suddenly, under stress, you fall back into old patterns. This moment is not a failure but an opportunity for deeper learning. Understanding that setbacks are standard growth parts can help you maintain momentum even when progress feels elusive. These moments often contain valuable lessons about your triggers and areas needing additional attention.

Setbacks in attachment healing are not only expected but can be valuable learning opportunities when approached with self-compassion and curiosity. The path to earned secure attachment often includes regression periods, particularly during stress or significant life changes. Understanding this natural ebb and flow helps maintain perspective during challenging periods.

Emma's experience illustrates this dynamic. After months of progress in managing her anxious attachment patterns, a job loss triggered old abandonment fears in her relationship. Initially, she felt devastated by what she perceived as "falling back" into previous patterns. However, working with her therapist, she came to understand that setbacks often contain important information about unresolved attachment needs and remaining growth areas.

The key difference between early recovery and later setbacks lies in developing awareness and tools. While the emotional intensity might feel similar, those who have done attachment work typically recover more quickly and can more effectively identify triggers. This awareness allows for faster implementation of coping strategies and a return to security.

During setbacks, the brain's threat response system can temporarily override newer, more secure attachment patterns. Understanding this neurobiological response helps reduce shame and enables a more constructive approach to recovery. The goal shifts from preventing all setbacks to building stronger recovery muscles.

Creating a setback response plan before challenges arise can provide a crucial roadmap during difficult times. This plan might include identifying early warning signs, establishing communication protocols with key supporters, and outlining specific self-care practices that have proven effective. Regular review and updating of this plan strengthens its effectiveness.

The concept of "productive regression" suggests that sometimes, moving backward temporarily allows for more profound healing. These periods often reveal subtle patterns that were not visible before, offering opportunities for a more complete resolution of attachment wounds. Viewing setbacks through this lens transforms them from failures into stepping stones toward greater security.

BUILDING RESILIENCE THROUGH CHALLENGES

Each challenge in your healing journey builds resilience, like a muscle growing stronger through exercise. Consider the story of Lisa, who faced intense anxiety when attempting to form new relationships. Rather than avoiding connections entirely, she learned to view each interaction as practice in building resilience. In six months, she developed a toolkit of coping strategies, transforming challenges into opportunities for growth. This resilience became her foundation for maintaining progress even during difficult times.

Resilience in attachment work develops by facing and processing challenges rather than avoiding them. Successfully navigating difficulties builds confidence in our ability to maintain a connection through adversity. This process strengthens both individual capacity for regulation and relationship durability.

James discovered this while working through trust issues with his partner. Each time they successfully resolved a conflict, his nervous system recorded a new experience of repair and return to connection. Within months, these experiences created a foundation of resilience that helped him maintain perspective during triggering situations.

Developing attachment resilience involves strengthening both internal and external resources. Internal resources include emotional regulation skills, self-awareness, and cognitive flexibility. External resources encompass supportive relationships, professional help, and environmental factors promoting security. The interaction between these resources creates a robust support system for navigating challenges.

The concept of "stress inoculation" applies particularly well to attachment resilience. Gradually facing attachment challenges in a supported way helps build tolerance for relationship stress. This process must be calibrated carefully - too much challenge overwhelms the system, while too little provides insufficient opportunity for growth.

Creating a personal resilience inventory helps track growth and identify areas for development. This inventory might include successful navigation of past challenges, current coping strategies, and available support systems. Regular updates to this inventory provide concrete evidence of progress and help maintain motivation during difficult periods.

Advanced resilience is developing the capacity to connect with yourself while navigating relationship challenges. This dual awareness allows for emotional engagement and wise perspective, reducing the likelihood of becoming completely overwhelmed by attachment triggers.

I cannot overstate the role of community in building resilience. Connecting with others who understand attachment work provides validation, shared wisdom, and living examples of earned security. These connections create a broader context for individual healing and demonstrate the possibility of lasting change.

Time perspective plays a crucial role in building resilience. Understanding that healing follows a spiral rather than a linear path helps maintain hope during setbacks. Each return to familiar challenges brings new insights and opportunities for deeper integration of secure attachment patterns.

The ultimate goal of resilience building is not to eliminate all attachment anxiety or avoidance but to develop confidence in our ability to return to security. This confidence comes from repeated experiences of successfully navigating challenges and maintaining connection through difficulties. With time, this creates a foundational sense of security that can weather significant life challenges while maintaining healthy attachment bonds. In the next chapter, we will explore embracing a new relational identity and how these personal growth practices can transform our interactions with others.

MEASURING AND TRACKING PROGRESS

Understanding your growth in attachment healing requires both quantitative and qualitative measures. Progress often appears in subtle shifts—a calmer response to triggers, quicker recovery from attachment wounds, or increased comfort with emotional intimacy. Creating structured ways to track these changes helps validate your journey and identify areas needing attention.

Consider implementing these tracking methods:

1. **Weekly Attachment Journal**: Document specific interactions, emotional responses, and recovery times from triggering events
2. **Monthly Security Scale**: Rate your sense of security in relationships across different domains (1-10 scale)
3. **Relationship Pattern Tracking**: Note the frequency of secure versus insecure responses to everyday situations
4. **Recovery Time Log**: Monitor how quickly you return to baseline after attachment triggers
5. **Connection Capacity Chart**: Track duration and quality of emotional intimacy in relationships

Sarah's experience illustrates effective progress tracking. She maintained a detailed journal of her attachment responses, noting that her recovery time from abandonment triggers decreased from days to hours over six months. This concrete evidence of progress helped maintain motivation during challenging periods.

CHAPTER 10
EMBRACING A NEW RELATIONAL IDENTITY

IMAGINE WAKING UP ONE MORNING AND DECIDING TO WEAR A NEW pair of glasses through which you view the world. Everything appears more precise and more vibrant, and the contours of your surroundings take on a refreshed significance. This act of clarity parallels the process of redefining your relational identity. Just as glasses can correct vision, embracing a new relational identity can transform how you perceive and engage in relationships. It is about stepping back and examining the roles you have unconsciously assumed, the labels you have worn, and deciding which ones to keep and which to shed. For those healing from disorganized attachment, embracing a new relational identity involves integrating seemingly contradictory aspects of self—the part that yearns for connection and the part that fears it. This integration is essential to developing a coherent sense of self in relationships, empowering you to take control of your relational journey.

UNDERSTANDING AND CRAFTING YOUR RELATIONAL IDENTITY

Relational identity is the self-concept you hold in the context of relationships. It encompasses how you see yourself, believe others see you, and your roles in your interactions. Past relationships often shape this identity, carrying the imprints of joyful and painful experiences. Perhaps you have been the caregiver, always putting others first, or the peacemaker, smoothing conflicts. These roles, while familiar, can limit your growth and fulfillment if not consciously examined. Recognizing these patterns is the first step in understanding how they influence your current self. Acknowledging their origins can redefine your identity to align with your true self and desires.

Crafting a new relational identity is a conscious and deliberate process. Start by identifying your core beliefs and values. These guiding principles define what matters most to you in relationships. Consider what qualities you admire in others and wish to embody yourself. Next, envision your ideal relational self. Picture how you want to interact with others—are you more assertive, compassionate, or open? This vision acts as a compass, directing your relationship behaviors and decisions. Setting clear intentions allows you to step confidently into this new identity, shedding roles that no longer serve you. When crafting a new relational identity after disorganized attachment, it is essential to acknowledge the protective function of old patterns and the possibility of new, more secure ways of relating. This involves gradually expanding your "window of tolerance for emotional intimacy," which refers to the range of emotional experiences you can comfortably manage. Expanding this window allows you to engage in deeper, more fulfilling relationships. A wider window will enable you to handle more intense emotional interactions, leading to deeper, more fulfilling relationships.

Self-perception plays a pivotal role in shaping your relational identity. How you view yourself influences your interactions and expectations in relationships. A positive self-image attracts compatible partners who resonate with your true self. Conversely, a negative self-view might lead you to accept less than you deserve. Understanding your self-concept clarity—the extent to which your self-beliefs are clearly defined and consistent—can enhance relationship satisfaction and commitment. You create healthier, more fulfilling connections by cultivating a clear and positive self-view and realizing the power of your thoughts and beliefs in shaping your relational journey. This empowerment allows you to take control of your relationships and foster personal growth.

To support this identity transformation, engage in exercises that align with your vision. One potent activity is writing a letter to your future self. In this letter, describe your ideal relational identity and your steps to achieve it. Reflect on the changes you wish to see and the emotions you hope to experience. This exercise solidifies your intentions and serves as a source of motivation and guidance. Another effective tool is creating a vision board for your relational goals. Use images, words, and symbols representing the qualities and relationships you aspire to cultivate. Place this board somewhere visible to remind you of your journey and keep you focused on your path. And once again, practicing mindfulness can help you stay present in your relationships and align your actions with your desired identity. Reflecting on your interactions at the end of each day can also provide valuable insights and help you track your progress.

Reflection Section: Craft Your Relational Identity

Take a moment to reflect on your current relational identity. What roles and labels have you unconsciously adopted? For instance, you might see yourself as the "caretaker" who always puts others' needs before your own or the "people-pleaser" who avoids conflict at all costs. How do these roles impact your interactions and relationships? Write down your core values and envision your ideal relational self. Consider making a vision board or writing a letter to your future self-detailing your desired relational identity. This exercise will help clarify your intentions and guide you in redefining your relational identity for personal growth and fulfillment.

CELEBRATING PROGRESS AND MILESTONES

Imagine standing at the top of a hill, gazing back at the winding path you have traversed. Each step forward, each challenge overcome, represents the progress you have made. We often forget to pause and appreciate these milestones in our personal growth. Yet, acknowledging achievements is vital. It motivates you and boosts self-esteem, reinforcing the positive changes you have worked hard to achieve. For those with disorganized attachment histories, celebrating progress might initially feel threatening or unfamiliar. Starting with small, private acknowledgments can help build comfort with recognition and success. When you take the time to celebrate, you affirm these changes, making them a permanent part of your identity. This celebration is not just about the significant victories. It is about recognizing the small, everyday steps that contribute to your growth, each a building block in the foundation of your new self. By acknowledging your progress, you validate your efforts and recognize the steps you have taken toward personal growth, making you feel validated and recognized.

Reinforcing positive behaviors through celebration is like watering a plant; it encourages continued growth and resilience. Acknowledging your progress strengthens the neural pathways associated with positive behaviors, making them more likely to recur. This creates a cycle of positivity, where each success breeds further success. Celebrating these moments also boosts your confidence and morale. By recognizing your accomplishments, you remind yourself of your capabilities and potential. This self-assurance propels you forward, empowering you to tackle future challenges more easily. In essence, celebration is a powerful tool for fostering a growth-oriented mindset that embraces change and transformation.

There are many ways to recognize and celebrate milestones in your journey. Journaling personal achievements is a simple yet effective method. By documenting your progress, you create a tangible record of your growth, one you can revisit whenever you need a boost of motivation. This practice helps you track your development and provides insight into the patterns and habits contributing to your success. Sharing these milestones with supportive friends or family amplifies their impact. When you involve others in your celebration, you create a sense of community and accountability. These shared moments of joy strengthen your relationships, reminding you that you are not alone in your quest for growth.

Acknowledging progress has profound psychological benefits. It enhances your well-being and commitment to change by reinforcing your efforts and encouraging further development. Celebrations strengthen the neural pathways for positive behavior, making these actions more automatic and ingrained. This neurological reinforcement is crucial for sustaining long-term growth, as it helps you internalize the changes you wish to see. By celebrating your achievements, you create a feedback loop of positivity, where each acknowledgment fuels further motivation and dedication.

Consider the story of Leanne, who marked her personal growth by hosting a small gathering of close friends. She shared her journey, highlighting the challenges she had overcome and the lessons she had learned. This celebration affirmed her progress and inspired her friends to embark on their paths of self-discovery. Another example is Justin, who reflected on his development through art. He created a series of paintings representing different aspects of his growth, each piece a visual testament to his transformation. These stories illustrate the diverse ways we can celebrate our achievements, using creativity and community to honor our progress.

Reflection Section: Celebrate Your Milestones

Reflect on your recent achievements, big or small. Consider how you can celebrate these milestones meaningfully. You might journal your progress, share it with a friend, or create something tangible to commemorate your journey. Remember, celebration is not a luxury but a vital part of personal growth. It reinforces the positive changes you have made and motivates you to continue on your path of transformation.

BUILDING A SUPPORTIVE COMMUNITY

Imagine a garden thriving with diverse plants, each contributing to the ecosystem as a garden flourishes with variety and personal growth blossoms within a supportive community. A network of encouraging people offers a fertile ground for development and resilience. Friends, family, and even mentors provide the accountability that keeps us on track. They cheer our victories and nudge us forward when we falter. This collective journey nurtures a sense of connection, a reminder that we are not alone. Through these relationships, insights are exchanged, and experiences are shared, enriching our understanding and broadening our perspectives. Building community can be particularly challenging for those with disorganized attachment, as trust and consistency may feel foreign. Starting with structured, time-limited interactions can help develop comfort with sustained connection.

Identifying and cultivating supportive relationships requires intention. Begin by seeking out groups or clubs that resonate with your interests. Whether it is a book club, a sports team, or an art class, these gatherings are fertile ground for forming connections with like-minded individuals. Such settings encourage exchanging ideas and experiences, sparking inspiration and camaraderie. Additionally, consider seeking out mentors or role models who embody the qualities you aspire to nurture. Their guidance and wisdom can be invaluable as you navigate your path. Building a community is not just about finding support; it is about contributing to the lives of others and creating a reciprocal flow of encouragement and growth.

A community rich in diverse perspectives enhances understanding and empathy. Interacting with people from various backgrounds and experiences challenges our assumptions and broadens our worldview. It encourages open dialogue, where differing opinions can coexist and enrich the conversation. This exchange fosters shared learning; each person brings unique insights and stories. Embracing these differences deepens our empathy and strengthens our ability to connect with others meaningfully. Engaging with diverse perspectives creates a more inclusive and compassionate approach to our relationships and personal growth.

To strengthen community bonds, consider organizing regular meet-ups or discussions. These gatherings, such as a monthly coffee chat or a book club meeting, can be informal. The key is to create a space where open dialogue and connection can flourish. Another way to deepen relationships within your community is by participating in group challenges or projects. Whether it is a volunteer initiative, a creative collaboration, or a fitness goal, working together toward a common objective fosters a sense of unity and shared purpose. These activities strengthen bonds and provide opportunities for people to learn from one another, enhancing the group's collective growth.

Interactive Element: Strengthening Community Bonds

Consider organizing a monthly meet-up with friends or becoming part of a local club that matches your interests. Use these opportunities to engage in open discussions, share experiences, and learn from one another. Alternatively, propose a group challenge or project that encourages collaboration and shared goals. This exercise will help you build deeper connections within your community, fostering a supportive network that nurtures personal growth and development.

SUSTAINING CHANGE AND GROWTH

Imagine growth as a living entity that requires nurturing through consistent commitment and ongoing effort. Setting goals and feeling motivated at the start is easy, but sustaining that momentum calls for dedication. Actual change is not a one-time event but an ongoing process that unfolds over months and years. Setting long-term relational goals can anchor your growth, giving you a clear direction to aim for. These goals include improving communication skills, deepening emotional connections, and cultivating empathy. By having these targets, you create a roadmap for your relational development. This clarity helps keep you motivated and focused, reminding you of the larger picture when daily challenges arise.

Embracing lifelong learning and adaptation is equally vital. The world around us is in constant flux, and so are we. Being open to learning new strategies and adapting to changing circumstances ensures your growth remains dynamic and relevant. Continuous development fosters resilience, equipping you to handle whatever life throws your way. This adaptability is about being flexible and viewing change as an opportunity for further growth. When you approach life with a mindset that welcomes learning, you remain open to new experiences and insights, enhancing your ability to sustain change over time.

Regularly revisiting your goals and values is crucial to maintain momentum in personal growth. Reflect on what truly matters to you and whether your current path aligns with those priorities. Periodic self-assessment helps you stay on track and make necessary adjustments. This reflection is not just about looking back; it is about looking forward and ensuring that your actions are aligned with your aspirations. Engaging in self-assessment allows you to identify areas that need attention and celebrate the progress you have made. It keeps you grounded and focused, providing the clarity needed to navigate the complexities of personal growth.

Adaptability plays a significant role in sustaining change, allowing you to adjust your goals in response to new experiences or insights. Life is unpredictable, and the growth path often has unexpected twists and turns. Being flexible enables you to embrace and use these changes to your advantage. When encountering new opportunities or challenges, reassess your goals and consider how they might evolve. This willingness to adapt ensures that your growth remains relevant and meaningful, allowing you to continue moving forward even when circumstances shift.

Consider the story of Alexander, who initially set out to improve his relationships by becoming a better listener. As he practiced and refined his skills, he discovered a passion for communication and decided to pursue a career in counseling. This unexpected path required him to adjust his goals, but his adaptability allowed him to thrive in this new direction. Additionally, consider Maia, who faced the challenge of relocating to a new city. Instead of viewing it as a setback, she saw it as an opportunity to explore different cultures and perspectives. By maintaining a growth mindset, Maia continued to seek new challenges and opportunities, enriching her personal and relational development.

Those healing from disorganized attachment often need to balance pushing for growth with maintaining emotional safety. This might mean progressing in smaller steps while building internal security. Sustaining change and growth is an ongoing process that requires a willingness to learn, dedication, and adaptability. By setting long-term goals, engaging in self-assessment, and remaining open to change, you can maintain momentum and ensure your growth journey is fulfilling and enduring. As you continue to embrace this dynamic process, remember that growth is not a destination but an evolving journey that unfolds with each step you take.

EMBRACING LASTING LOVE AND SECURITY

Imagine a relationship as a well-built house, standing firm against the tests of time and weather. Lasting love and security form the sturdy framework of this house, offering shelter and warmth. They are not fleeting emotions but enduring states that provide a stable foundation for the lives built within. Mutual respect and understanding are the cornerstones, supporting the structure with a balance of give-and-take. This mutual respect means valuing each other's perspectives and honoring individual differences, while understanding is deeply knowing and accepting each other's inner worlds. Together, they create an environment where both partners feel seen, heard, and valued, nurturing a bond that withstands life's inevitable storms.

Enduring love and security are also about trust and support, the beams that hold the house together. Trust is the unwavering belief in each other's integrity and intentions. It allows for vulnerability without fear of judgment or betrayal. Support is the steadfast presence that reassures both partners they are not alone. When trust and support are woven into the fabric of a relationship, they provide a sense of safety that encourages exploration and growth. This security creates a haven where both partners can express themselves freely and pursue their aspirations, knowing they have a reliable partner. For individuals working through disorganized attachment patterns, embracing lasting love involves learning to trust their capacity for secure attachment and their partner's consistency. This includes developing tolerance for positive experiences and learning to maintain connection during triggering moments.

As we have seen, consistent communication and emotional availability are key traits of relationships that embody lasting love. Think of these as our metaphorical house's open windows and doors, allowing light and fresh air to flow freely. Regular communication keeps everyone aligned, reducing misunderstandings and fostering harmony. It involves not just talking but actively listening and engaging in meaningful conversations. Emotional availability means being present for each other, offering empathy and understanding without judgment. When both partners are emotionally available, they create an environment where feelings can be expressed safely, deepening the emotional connection and trust.

Shared values and long-term commitment are like the solid roof that shelters the house. Shared values provide a common ground and a guiding compass that aligns the couple's goals and aspirations. They ensure that both partners move in the same direction, reinforcing the bond with shared purpose and meaning. Long-term commitment is the promise to weather life's ups and downs together. It is the conscious decision to invest in the relationship, nurturing it through attention, care, and effort. This commitment is not just a vow but a daily choice, a testament to the enduring nature of their love.

To cultivate lasting love and security, it is important to prioritize quality time and shared experiences. These moments add color and warmth to the relationship, creating memories that strengthen the bond. Prioritizing quality time means setting aside distractions and focusing on each other, whether through simple activities like cooking together or exploring new places. Shared experiences deepen the connection by fostering a sense of adventure and discovery. They remind both partners of the joy and excitement that brought them together, reinforcing the bond with shared laughter and wonder.

Continually investing in personal and relational growth is essential for nurturing enduring relationships. This means recognizing that growth is an ongoing process requiring dedication and effort. Personal growth involves self-reflection and self-improvement, ensuring both people bring their best selves to the relationship. Relational growth means actively working on communication, trust, and understanding, addressing challenges with empathy and collaboration. By valuing growth, both partners ensure that their relationship evolves and adapts, remaining resilient and fulfilling over a lifetime.

Consider the story of Anastasia and Nathan, who celebrated their anniversaries with meaningful traditions. Each year, they revisited where they first met, reflecting on their journey together and renewing their commitment to each other. These traditions became cherished rituals, reinforcing their bond with love and nostalgia. Another example is Ellen and Elliot, who supported each other through life's challenges. When Elliot faced a career setback, Ellen provided unwavering encouragement and belief in his abilities. This support strengthened their relationship, proving that love is not just about sharing the good times but standing by each other in adversity. These stories illustrate the power of lasting love, showing that relationships can thrive across a lifetime with mutual respect, understanding, and commitment.

CHAPTER 11
SEEKING PROFESSIONAL SUPPORT

THE JOURNEY OF HEALING ATTACHMENT WOUNDS SOMETIMES REQUIRES more than self-help strategies and personal reflection. Like a skilled navigator helping you chart unknown waters, a mental health professional plays a crucial role in your healing journey. They can provide expertise, guidance, and support that catalyzes profound healing. This chapter explores the vital role of professional support in attachment healing, helping you understand when and how to seek help, what types of therapy might benefit you, and how to make the most of therapeutic relationships. Remember, seeking help is not admitting failure but a courageous step toward growth and healing. For those with disorganized attachment, professional support is particularly crucial as healing often requires help in integrating contradictory survival responses and processing complex trauma. The therapeutic relationship can provide the consistent, regulated presence needed to develop earned, secure attachment.

WHEN TO SEEK PROFESSIONAL HELP

Imagine waking up each morning feeling like you are wearing emotional armor that has grown too heavy to bear. You have read self-help books, practiced mindfulness, and worked on personal growth, yet something still feels unresolved. This experience is common for those with attachment wounds, and recognizing when to seek professional help is crucial in your healing journey. The relief that comes with this recognition is immense, as it validates your experiences and reassures you that you are not alone. Being proactive and recognizing signs indicating professional help is essential, as they often signal the need for professional intervention.

Consider Maria's story: She managed her attachment issues independently for years, using meditation and journaling to cope with relationship anxiety. However, when a new romantic relationship triggered overwhelming fears of abandonment, she found herself unable to sleep, constantly checking her partner's social media, and experiencing panic attacks. These symptoms signaled that professional support could offer tools and perspectives beyond her coping strategies. Similarly, James realized he needed help when his difficulty trusting others began affecting his career advancement, preventing him from forming necessary professional relationships despite his technical expertise.

Those with disorganized attachment may notice additional signs like:

- Simultaneously craving and fearing close relationships

- Experiencing freeze responses during emotional intimacy
- Difficulty maintaining consistent feelings toward others
- Experiencing both anxious and avoidant behaviors
- Struggling with emotional regulation in relationships

Other key indicators that professional help might be beneficial include the following:

- Ongoing emotional distress that disrupts daily life
- Recurring relationship patterns that you cannot seem to break
- Intrusive thoughts or memories about past trauma
- Difficulty maintaining healthy boundaries
- Physical symptoms of anxiety or depression
- Feeling stuck despite implementing self-help strategies
- Isolation or withdrawal from relationships
- Overwhelming emotional responses to ordinary situations

The decision to seek help often involves hesitation and questions. You might wonder if your problems are "serious enough" to warrant professional intervention, or perhaps you feel shame about needing support. These concerns are typical but should not prevent you from seeking help. Remember, seeking help is not admitting failure but a courageous step toward growth and healing. Expert support can provide meaningful insights and helpful resources at any stage of your healing journey, whether you are just beginning to understand your attachment style or working to maintain progress in your relationships.

TYPES OF THERAPY FOR ATTACHMENT ISSUES

The therapeutic landscape offers a variety of approaches to healing attachment wounds, each with its unique benefits and methodologies. Understanding these options is crucial as it can help you make well-informed choices about your healing journey. For disorganized attachment, therapeutic approaches that specifically address trauma and dissociation are often the most effective. It is essential to understand these different types of therapy, as it will empower you to choose the one that best suits your needs and offers unique benefits for your healing journey:

1. **Sensorimotor Psychotherapy**: This form of somatic therapy focuses on healing disorganized attachment by integrating body-based interventions with psychological processing. This approach recognizes that traumatic experiences are stored in our body's nervous system and movement patterns. Therapists help us explore and renegotiate physical sensations and impulses associated with attachment wounds, allowing for gentle, bottom-up healing that supports nervous system regulation and creates new embodied experiences of safety and connection.

2. **Internal Family Systems**: IFS addresses disorganized attachment by understanding our internal psychological system as composed of multiple "parts" with different roles and protective functions. In this approach, the therapist helps us identify and compassionately engage with protective parts that developed in response to attachment trauma. This facilitates healing by accessing

our core "self"—an inherently whole and healing aspect that can integrate fragmented inner experiences and restore emotional balance and relational capacity.

3. **Dialectical Behavior Therapy**: DBT addresses disorganized attachment, providing skills in emotional regulation, distress tolerance, and interpersonal effectiveness. Therapists help us develop mindfulness and self-validation techniques that counteract the invalidating experiences often associated with early attachment trauma. By teaching us to recognize and modulate intense emotional responses, DBT supports healing attachment wounds through improved emotional resilience, more adaptive coping strategies, and the gradual development of healthier relational patterns.

These approaches help integrate fragmented aspects of experience and build coherent narrative understanding. Other therapies include the following:

1. **Cognitive Behavioral Therapy**: CBT focuses on identifying and changing thought patterns and behaviors that maintain attachment insecurities. This approach helps us recognize how early experiences shape our current relationship beliefs and provides practical tools for creating new, healthier patterns. For example, Cindy worked with a CBT therapist to challenge her belief that she was inherently unlovable. She learned to identify negative thought patterns through structured exercises and homework assignments and replace them with more balanced perspectives.

2. **Eye Movement Desensitization and Reprocessing**: This may be particularly effective for processing traumatic experiences that contribute to attachment issues. This therapy uses bilateral stimulation (typically eye movements) while processing difficult memories, helping to reduce their emotional impact. Peter, who experienced childhood neglect, found that EMDR helped him process these experiences in a way that talk therapy alone had not achieved. The treatment allowed him to integrate these memories without becoming overwhelmed by them.

3. **Psychodynamic Therapy**: This approach explores how past relationships and early experiences influence current attachment patterns. It helps us understand the unconscious motivations behind our behaviors and emotions in relationships. This deeper understanding allows us to make different choices in our current relationships. It provides a safe space to explore painful experiences and feelings while developing new ways of relating to others.

4. **Attachment-Based Therapy**: This approach, specifically designed to address attachment issues, focuses on creating a secure therapeutic relationship as a foundation for healing. The therapist serves as a safe base from which we can explore our attachment patterns and experiment with new ways of relating. This therapy helps us understand how our attachment style developed and provides opportunities to experience secure attachment within the therapeutic relationship.

5. **Group Therapy**: This offers unique benefits for attachment healing. It provides opportunities to practice

new relationship skills in a supportive environment. Witnessing others' experiences and receiving feedback from peers can provide valuable insights and normalize our struggles. The group setting allows us to explore attachment patterns in real time while developing healthy relationships with other group members.

WORKING WITH THERAPISTS

The relationship with your therapist is a powerful catalyst for healing attachment wounds. Like learning to dance with a skilled partner, working with a therapist requires trust, communication, and willingness to try new steps. The process begins with finding the right therapist who understands attachment theory and creates a safe space for exploration and growth. When healing from disorganized attachment, seeing a therapist experienced in complex trauma is essential. The therapeutic relationship may initially feel threatening, and a skilled therapist will gradually understand how to build safety while respecting protective responses.

1. **Finding the Right Fit**: The search for a therapist might feel overwhelming, but consider it an investment in your healing journey. Start by researching people who specialize in attachment issues or trauma. Many offer initial consultations, during which you can assess their approach and your comfort level with them. Pay attention to your feelings in their presence: Do you feel heard and understood? Do they explain their approach clearly? Trust your instincts while remaining open to the process.

2. **Building the Therapeutic Alliance**: A strong therapeutic relationship develops gradually, like any secure attachment. Your therapist should demonstrate consistency, empathy, and professional boundaries while creating space for you to explore difficult emotions. This relationship can become a template for secure attachment, showing you what it feels like to have a reliable, attuned presence in your life.

3. **Navigating Challenges**: Therapeutic work often stirs up difficult emotions and resistance. Especially when working on core attachment wounds, you might feel vulnerable, defensive, or tempted to withdraw. These reactions are normal and can provide valuable information about your attachment patterns. A skilled therapist will help you navigate these challenges while maintaining a safe therapeutic environment.

MAKING THE MOST OF THERAPY

Therapy is an investment in your emotional well-being, and like any investment, its success depends partly on how you engage with the process. Think of therapy as a collaborative journey where you and your therapist contribute to the healing process. Your active participation can significantly enhance the benefits you receive from therapy.

1. **Between-Session Work**: Therapy's impact extends beyond the session hour through homework assignments, journaling, or practicing new skills. These activities help integrate therapeutic insights into your daily life. For

instance, Elena's therapist suggested she keep a relationship journal, noting situations that triggered attachment anxiety and her responses. This practice helped her identify patterns and apply therapeutic tools in real time.

2. **Setting Goals and Tracking Progress**: Clear therapeutic goals help you focus your work and measure progress. These goals might include developing better boundaries, reducing anxiety in relationships, or processing specific traumas. Regularly reviewing these goals with your therapist ensures your work aligns with your healing objectives. Remember that progress is often not linear; setbacks are standard parts of the healing journey. For those with disorganized attachment, progress usually involves learning to tolerate positive experiences and connections. Small steps toward consistency and emotional regulation are significant achievements worth noting.

3. **Integration and Application**: The real work of therapy happens as you apply insights and skills in your daily life. This might involve practicing new communication patterns in relationships, setting boundaries with family members, or using self-soothing techniques during moments of attachment activation. Each small step builds confidence and creates new neural pathways for secure attachment.

ALTERNATIVE SUPPORT RESOURCES

Beyond traditional therapy, various resources can complement your healing journey. These alternatives provide different perspectives and support levels, creating a comprehensive healing approach.

1. **Support Groups**:

   - Online and in-person attachment-focused groups
   - Adult Children of Dysfunctional Families (ACoA) meetings
   - Trauma survivor groups
   - Relationship skills workshops

2. **Online Communities**:

   - Moderated forums for attachment healing
   - Social media groups focused on secure attachment
   - Virtual support circles
   - Educational platforms with attachment-focused content

3. **Workshops and Retreats**:

   - Attachment healing intensives
   - Relationship skills workshops
   - Body-based trauma workshops
   - Mindfulness retreats for attachment work

CREATING A SUPPORT TEAM

Building an adequate support network requires coordination and clear communication between different resources. Think of your support team as collaborative, with each member contributing unique perspectives and support.

Core Team Components

1. **Primary Therapist**:

   - Coordinates overall treatment
   - Provides individual support
   - Guides therapeutic process

2. **Support Groups**:

   - Offer peer understanding
   - Provide regular connection
   - Share coping strategies

3. **Personal Relationships**:

   - Trusted friends/family
   - Partner(s)
   - Mentors

Coordination Strategies:

   - Regular check-ins with each support source

- Clear communication about boundaries and roles
- Integration of different perspectives and tools
- Periodic team assessment and adjustment

For example, Maya coordinates with her therapist, attachment support group, and trusted friend. Her therapist helps process deeper issues, her support group provides weekly connections, and her friend offers practical support. This coordinated approach provides comprehensive support for her healing journey.

CONCLUSION

As you reach the end of this book, reflect on your journey from disorganized attachment to secure attachment. Each chapter has been a step on this path, guiding you through understanding your attachment style, recognizing emotional triggers, building trust, and transforming relationships. You have explored how emotional regulation, self-worth, and effective communication can lead to profound personal growth and healthier connections. This transformation is within your grasp, and the tools and insights you have gained are your compass.

Attachment theory offers a foundation for understanding how early experiences shape our relationships. Understanding these concepts opens the door to personal growth. Emotional regulation and trust-building are the bedrock of secure relationships. As you have learned, transforming relationship patterns involves recognizing and breaking free from toxic dynamics. Self-worth and self-compassion are crucial for building a strong foundation, and effective communication is the bridge that connects us to others.

Throughout this book, you have uncovered key takeaways to guide your journey. You have learned to identify emotional triggers and regulate your responses. Mindfulness and cognitive restructuring have offered ways to balance emotions. Trust-building and breaking unhealthy patterns have paved the way for stronger connections. You have embraced self-worth and self-compassion, setting the stage for lasting love. Each chapter has equipped you with practical strategies to foster secure attachments.

Take a moment to celebrate your progress. Your courage and resilience in embarking on this journey are commendable. Embracing a new relational identity is a significant achievement. Each milestone is a testament to your growth, no matter how small. Reflect on how far you have come and the potential that lies ahead. Your journey is not just about what you have achieved so far but about the continuous potential for growth and change.

Remember, this journey is not just about what you've achieved. It is about applying the tools and strategies you have learned every day. Your commitment to personal growth and securing fulfilling relationships is key. Let the insights and practices from this book guide your daily interactions and nurture the connections you value. Your commitment is the driving force behind your success.

Also, remember that ongoing practice and reflection are essential to sustaining change. Make habits like gratitude journaling, and mindfulness exercises a part of your daily routine. Regular self-assessment will keep you aligned with your goals. These practices will help you stay connected and grounded in your journey. Remember, growth is a continuous process that requires dedication, but the rewards are worth it.

You are not alone in this journey. Share your experiences and insights with others. Engaging with a supportive community will encourage you and give you new perspectives. Seek out groups or forums to connect with others on similar paths. These connections can enrich your journey and offer a sense of belonging. Remember, you have a community of support around you as you continue to secure attachment, and your experiences can also inspire others on their journey.

Hold on to hope and inspiration as you continue this journey. Secure attachment can profoundly impact your relationships and overall well-being. With dedication and self-awareness, lasting love and security are attainable. You have the power to create fulfilling connections that enrich your life.

I am deeply grateful that you have trusted this book as a companion on your journey. We share the goal of achieving secure and loving relationships. Your engagement with the material and commitment to personal growth are genuinely inspiring. Thank you for allowing me to be part of your path to transformation.

As you close this book, feel empowered to make lasting changes. Embrace your new relational identity and continue striving for personal and relational fulfillment. The steps you have taken are just the beginning. Your journey toward secure attachment is a path of continuous discovery and growth. May it lead you to the love and security you deserve, and remember, your growth potential is limitless.

FURTHER READING

Attachment Theory, Bowlby's Stages & Attachment Styles, https://positivepsychology.com/attachment-theory/

Transcending childhood trauma in adult relationships, https://www.counselling-directory.org.uk/articles/transcending-childhood-trauma-in-adult-relationships/

Disorganized Attachment: Definition, Causes, & Signs, https://www.choosingtherapy.com/disorganized-attachment/

Mary Ainsworth: Attachment Theory and the Strange Situation, https://www.attachmentproject.com/attachment-theory/mary-ainsworth/

How to Heal Disorganized Attachment: Self-Regulation Tips, https://www.attachmentproject.com/blog/self-regulation-disorganized-attachment-triggers/

Mindfulness and Emotion Regulation, https://pmc.ncbi.nlm.nih.gov/articles/PMC5337506/

Cognitive Restructuring: Techniques and Examples, https://www.healthline.com/health/cognitive-restructuring/

Building Resilience With Mindfulness-Based Stress Reduction, https://www.apa.org/ed/precollege/topss/stress-reduction.pdf/

The Effect of Early Traumatic Experiences and Adult Attachment on Parental Reflective Functioning, https://pmc.ncbi.nlm.nih.gov/articles/PMC5364177/

20 Ways to Rebuild Trust in a Relationship, https://www.choosingtherapy.com/how-to-rebuild-trust/

Understanding Fear of Abandonment, https://www.verywellmind.com/fear-of-abandonment-2671741/

Setting Healthy Boundaries in Relationships, https://www.helpguide.org/relationships/social-connection/setting-healthy-boundaries-in-relationships/

Toxic Relationships Checklist, https://www.mindfulecotherapycenter.com/wp-content/uploads/2017/01/Toxic-Relationships-Checklist.pdf/

What Are the Short- and Long-Term Effects of Emotional Abuse?, https://www.healthline.com/health/mental-health/effects-of-emotional-abuse/

7 Ways to Improve Communication in Relationships, https://positivepsychology.com/communication-in-relationships/

Breaking the Pattern of Painful, Unhealthy Relationships, https://tinybuddha. com/blog/breaking-the-pattern-of-painful-unhealthy-relationships/

Self-Compassion Research, https://self-compassion.org/the-research/

How Gratitude Changes You and Your Brain, https://greatergood.berkeley.edu/ article/item/how_gratitude_changes_you_and_your_brain/

Neural mechanisms of self-affirmation's stress buffering effects, https://academic.oup.com/scan/article/15/10/1086/5815969/

Self Acceptance Therapy: Embrace Your True Self, https://ca4wellbeing.com/self-acceptance-therapy/

An Attachment Theory Perspective on Closeness and Intimacy, https://labs.psych. ucsb.edu/collins/nancy/UCSB_Close_Relationships_Lab/Publications_files/ CollinsFeeney%282004%29-Chapter3.pdf/

14 Proven Ways To Build Emotional Intimacy In 2024, https://practicalintimacy. com/how-to-build-emotional-intimacy-relationship/

How to Balance Independence & Healthy Relationships, https:// mindfulhealthsolutions.com/how-to-balance-your-independence-and-interdependence-for-healthy-relationships/

Active Listening in Relationships: A Path To Deeper Intimacy, https:// holdinghopemft.com/active-listening-a-key-to-deeper-intimacy-and-understanding-in-your-relationship

How to Express Emotions: 12 Ways to Communicate Feelings, https:// positivepsychology.com/express-emotions/

5 Conflict Resolution Strategies, https://www.pon.harvard.edu/daily/conflict-resolution/conflict-resolution-strategies/

Improving Emotional Intelligence (EQ): Expert Guide, https://www.helpguide. org/mental-health/wellbeing/emotional-intelligence-eq/

Secure Attachment: Signs, Benefits, and How to Cultivate It, https://www. verywellmind.com/secure-attachment-signs-benefits-and-how-to-cultivate-it-8628802/

How to Develop a Secure Attachment Style, https://blog.zencare.co/how-to-develop-a-secure-attachment-style/

Relationship Influences on Exploration in Adulthood, https://pmc.ncbi.nlm.nih. gov/articles/PMC2805473/

6 Tips for Ending a Cycle of Unhealthy Relationships, https://www. psychologytoday.com/us/blog/conquering-codependency/202010/6-tips-ending-cycle-unhealthy-relationships/

The Impact of Daily Habits on Long-Term Success - Life Planner, https://

thelifeplanner.co/blog/post/the_impact_of_daily_habits_on_long_term_success.html/

Mindfulness for Your Health, https://newsinhealth.nih.gov/2021/06/mindfulness-your-health/

Self-Reflection: A Pathway to Personal Growth, https://www.linkedin.com/pulse/self-reflection-pathway-personal-growth-adil-mahmoud/

The Transformative Power of Gratitude: A Path To Personal Resilience, https://www.forbes.com/sites/chriswestfall/2024/11/28/the-transformative-power-of-gratitude-a-path-to-personal-resilience/

Disorganized Attachment Style in a Relationship, https://www.thecouplescenter.org/disorganized-attachment-style-in-a-relationship/

Secure Attachment: Signs, Benefits, and How to Cultivate It, https://www.verywellmind.com/secure-attachment-signs-benefits-and-how-to-cultivate-it-8628802/

The Role of Self-concept Clarity in Relationship Quality, https://www.tandfonline.com/doi/full/10.1080/15298860903332191/

How Community Support Fuels Personal Growth, https://advantagecaregroup.org/2023/12/29/building-stronger-together-how-community-support-fuels-personal-growth/

www.ingramcontent.com/pod-product-compliance
Lightning Source LLC
Chambersburg PA
CBHW071747120626
46550CB00002B/694